PETER GREENAWAY

PETER GREENAWAY
ARCHITECTURE AND ALLEGORY

BRIDGET ELLIOTT AND ANTHONY PURDY

A.D. ACADEMY EDITIONS

For Zoë

ACKNOWLEDGEMENTS

This book would not have been possible without the help of Peter Greenaway, Eliza Poklewski Koziell and Nicola Kearton – to all of them our warmest thanks. For their discussions, comments, criticisms and support of various kinds, we thank David Clark, Julia Cook, Katy Emck, Amos Friedland, Mark Gorchynski, Brenda Jackson, Martin Lefebvre, Madeline Lennon, Paul Martin, Saman Musacchio, Dorit Naaman, Lucy Pribas, Chris Rechner, Habiba Sebkhi, and all the students of 'Crossed Cultures: Peter Greenaway and the Culture Industry', a cross-listed, team-taught interdisciplinary course given at the University of Alberta in 1994-95. Thanks, too, to the folks at the Toronto International Film Festival, Cinematheque Ontario and the Film Reference Library for inviting us to a press screening of *The Pillow Book* and making their archive available. Bridget Kinally at the BFI responded promptly and helpfully to all our long-distance enquiries, as did Elisabeth Lagune and Danièle Rivière at Dis Voir. We are grateful to the Smallman Fund at the University of Western Ontario for its generous help with plates. A special thank you goes to Jim Good, Dean of Arts at UWO, for his faith in the kind of work we do and his commitment to interdisciplinarity in both classroom and scholarship. Finally, thanks to Andrea Bettella (Art Editor), Mario Bettella (Chief Designer), Francesca Tommasi (Designer) and Ramona Khambatta (Editor) at Academy Editions.

Unless otherwise stated, all images are courtesy of Peter Greenaway © All Arts: pp8, 11, 13 (below), 15-16, 17, 71- 73, 82, 88 (above and below, left and right), 89, 106 photos: Marc Guillamot; pp9, 10 (above), 12 (above left and right), 30-32, 36-37, 90, 95 courtesy BFI Stills, Posters and Designs (London); pp12 (below), 19, 64-65, 68-69 courtesy Dis Voir (Paris); pp13 (above), 81, 89, 104, 105 photos: Stephen Pyke; pp20, 22-23 photos: Annaleen Louwes; p48 (above) public domain; p49 courtesy Witt Library, Courtauld Institute of Art, University of London (London); p54 courtesy Ashmoleon Museum (Oxford); p70 photo: Deen van Meer (Amsterdam); pp74, 76-77 photos: Eve Ramboz; pp83, 86 (above), 88 (centre), 94 photos: Manu Lukschs; pp86 (below), 87 (above) photos: Jannes Linders; p87 (below) photo: Peter Cox; pp80, 91, 96, 126 photos: Graham Matthews; p97 photo: Claudio Franzini

COVER: 'Pop-Up' Book of Architecture, Prospero's Books, 1991
PAGE 2: The Belly of an Architect, 1987

First published in Great Britain in 1997 by
ACADEMY EDITIONS
a division of John Wiley & Sons,
Baffins Lane, Chichester,
West Sussex PO19 1UD

Other Wiley Editorial Offices
New York • Weinheim • Brisbane • Singapore • Toronto

ISBN 0-471-97691-1

Printed and bound in Singapore

CONTENTS

INTRODUCTION

Born in Newport, Wales, in 1942, Peter Greenaway is one of the most innovative and controversial of contemporary filmmakers. Since his days at the Walthamstow College of Art, he has always thought of himself as a painter first and foremost and his work continues to be shown in galleries worldwide. His filmmaking apprenticeship was an unorthodox one, spent cutting documentaries for the Central Office of Information from 1965 to 1976. The subjects may not have been to his taste – basically British propaganda for export – but he learned to edit large amounts of often badly shot film very fast. In 1966 he began making short films of his own, influenced by the structuralism that was then effecting profound changes in many fields. These early films of the sixties and seventies already bore the Greenaway signature: a fondness for landscape; a fascination with lists, grids, taxonomies, catalogues, counting games and aleatory sequences; a parodic use of the documentary voice-over; and, above all, a quirky sense of humour that constantly reminded the viewer not to take things too seriously.

Since the critical success of *The Draughtsman's Contract*, released in 1982, Greenaway has become best known for his feature films: *A Zed & Two Noughts* (1986), *The Belly of an Architect* (1987), *Drowning by Numbers* (1988), *The Cook, the Thief, His Wife and Her Lover* (1989), *Prospero's Books* (1991), *The Baby of Mâcon* (1993) and *The Pillow Book* (1996). During the same period, he has done a considerable amount of work for television – for example, *Four American Composers* (1983), *Death in the Seine* (1988), *A TV Dante Cantos 1-8* (1989), *M is for Man, Music, Mozart* (1991) and *Darwin* (1992) – and has more recently ventured into opera with *Rosa, A Horse Drama*, performed in 1994 in Amsterdam. Of particular significance in the 1990s has been his curatorial work, with major exhibitions in several European cities: *The Physical Self* (Rotterdam, 1991), *100 Objects to Represent the World* (Vienna, 1992), *Le Bruit des Nuages – Flying Out of This World* (Paris, 1992), *Watching Water* (Venice, 1993), *Some Organising Principles* (Swansea, 1993), *The Audience of Mâcon* (Cardiff, 1993), *The Stairs/Geneva: The Location* (1994), *The Stairs/Munich: Projection* (1995), *In the Dark* (part of *Spellbound: Art and Film* at the Hayward Gallery in London, 1996).

The present book is not intended as an exhaustive account of Greenaway's extraordinarily varied production, which it makes no attempt to cover in an even way. (There is little discussion, for example, of the films for television or the painting, and the feature films are dealt with unequally according to the arguments being made.) For those who are not overly familiar with Greenaway's *œuvre* or who know only one aspect of it, the book will serve as an introduction both to the work itself and to the debates around it. For the rapidly growing number of devotees and serious students of Greenaway, it will present an analysis and a coherent set of arguments about the films and the curatorial exhibitions. The overall objective is to bring Greenaway's work to life for as large an audience as possible by situating it in relation to the broader cultural concerns of our time as they find expression in fields as diverse as architecture, cinema, literature and museology. We hope in the process to demystify a body of work that has at times been significantly misrepresented by critics more interested in scoring ideological points than in understanding what they are looking at.

Chapter 1 draws on Walter Benjamin's analysis of baroque allegory in order to situate Greenaway's artistic practice in relation to a neo-baroque aesthetic of display and excess. The chapter also explores the creation of a postmodern *Gesamtkunstwerk* involving complex forms of artistic collaboration and technological experiment. Chapter 2 offers a close reading of *The Draughtsman's Contract* and addresses Greenaway's use of allegory as a structuring device. The plots of history, art history and sexual politics are mapped onto one another to reveal an obscure allegory of transmission; as modes of knowing enter into conflict, it becomes apparent that the interpretation of material evidence is a function of the way that evidence is framed. Chapter 3 asks the question, What is the relationship between buildings and bodies? The question is a constant in Greenaway's work and its non-Vitruvian answer finds its most sustained expression in *The Belly of an Architect*. The film is examined here in the light not only of recent writing on architecture but also of Georges Bataille's disturbing juxtaposition of museum and slaughterhouse as the twin architectural figures of modernity.

Focusing on *The Cook, the Thief, His Wife and Her Lover*, *Prospero's Books* and *The Baby of Mâcon*, Chapter 4 considers how Greenaway uses theatrical structures and images to explore power relations between author, actor and audience. The role of the audience is foregrounded as Greenaway demands that his viewers consider the implications both of their own voyeurism and of the use and abuse of new technologies of representation. Chapter 5 examines Greenaway's curatorial work (and the curatorial impulse in films such as *Prospero's Books* and *The Pillow Book*) in the light of recent theoretical discussions of collecting as a form of control and containment. Greenaway's own fascination with encyclopedic systems and their limitations finds a logical extension in the ever-expanding curatorial projects by which he attempts to take both cinema and the museum out into the everyday life of the modern city. What sort of filmmaking niche does Greenaway occupy and why do his films tend to polarise audiences? The final chapter attempts to answer this question by charting how the critical response to Greenaway's films has evolved over the past fifteen years. More specifically, it examines indirect forms of censorship and assesses reviewers' complaints of violence and pornography, reactionary nostalgia and intellectual exhibitionism.

The book concludes with an interview with Greenaway that took place in October 1996. A filmography, a list of exhibitions and a bibliography are included at the end.

FOR THE SAKE OF THE CORPSE
Baroque Perspectives

BELOW
Alain Resnais, Last Year in Marienbad/
L'Année dernière à Marienbad, 1961

OPPOSITE
Prospero's Books, *still life with butterfly*

When questioned about his future plans during a 1987 interview, Peter Greenaway floated his proposal for a film entitled *The Stairs*. Although the film's baroque theme and scale would have sorely strained the budgetary limitations of alternative cinema, Greenaway's description of this unrealised (and perhaps unrealisable) project offers intriguing insights into his view of art. As he explained at the time, the film would tell the story of a young English painter who travels to Rome in order to recreate a huge baroque ceiling containing a host of allegorical figures and dazzling *trompe l'œil* effects. While in Rome, the painter (whom Greenaway describes as an unpleasant young man ruled more by his head than his heart – a charge sometimes levelled at Greenaway himself) decides to humiliate his critics by forging an Italian masterpiece. Claiming to have discovered Monteverdi's lost opera of the *Marriage of Aeneas*, he contrives to get himself appointed artistic director for the production of his own script. After mounting a highly successful performance with a cast of thousands, he reveals the hoax and causes an uproar. The American financiers withdraw their funding while the painter's personal enemies exact a more suitably baroque form of revenge by hiding his murdered corpse on his own ceiling. His body is so skilfully disguised as one of the painted figures that no suspicions are raised until the worms eating the painter's decaying flesh start falling to the ground.[1]

The proposal warrants our attention, not only because Greenaway revives it (albeit greatly modified) as a huge ongoing curatorial project, similarly entitled *The Stairs*, which we shall discuss in more detail in Chapter 5, but also because it foregrounds the more baroque aspects of Greenaway's cinema, including his passion for seventeenth-century settings, startling *trompe l'œil* visuals, and richly allegorical conceits of flight and fall, ambition and decay. *The Stairs*, as originally conceived, would have been a late twentieth-century *Gesamtkunstwerk* deriving its flaunted theatricality and powers of illusion from the latest developments in multimedia technology. The unrealised project provides a striking illustration of the delight Greenaway takes in probing and disrupting the binary legacy of a Western cultural tradition founded on careful distinctions between mind and body, male and female, culture and nature, high and low, art and kitsch. The filmmaker's pleasure is contagious as we are drawn into the darkly absurdist games he plays with fundamental structures of belief and systems of ordering and classification. Here, in *The Stairs*, an ascension has gone badly wrong. Instead of joyfully witnessing the risen body passing into eternal life, we see a corpse being maliciously hoisted to the ceiling in a supremely perverse gesture that ironically makes the painter one with his art – at least for as long as it takes for the precariously perched, worm-ridden body to succumb to the twin laws of gravity and decay and return to earth, ruining the ceiling in the process. As Greenaway notes, he wanted to 'use the story as a vehicle to explore tricks of cul-

ture, tricks of the cinema, tricks of painting'[2] – an ambition that remains constant throughout an œuvre characterised by its allegorical migrations across the arts and its fascination with every manner of illusion.

It should come as no great surprise that Greenaway's explorations are so often situated in the baroque seventeenth century, a period in which illusionist art was produced on an unprecedented scale for a relatively small number of powerful patrons from within the Roman Catholic Church and Europe's ruling houses. The word 'baroque' was originally a term of abuse used by eighteenth-century scholars to dismiss the work of the preceding century as bizarre, diseased and excessive to the point of ridicule. It has since been developed more seriously and more fully by art historians such as Heinrich Wölfflin, Henri Focillon and Eugenio d'Ors, whose studies strive to analyse certain morphological features that were considered antithetical to the values of classical art. Greatly influenced by Nietzsche's distinction between the Apollonian and the Dionysian, the modern art historical paradigm of a tension between classical and baroque is central to Greenaway's own exploration of the Western tradition. Baroque, too, is the fascination with allegorical and emblematic devices, as we see in the extended analogy developed in the *Stairs* proposal between painting and filmmaking. Although such devices appeared long before the baroque period proper, Walter Benjamin has argued that the art of allegory reached new heights in the melancholy strains of a turbulent seventeenth century, which both he and Greenaway have compared with our own century in certain aspects of its cultural production.

Any discussion of baroque revivals needs to address (however briefly and sketchily) how the baroque has been variously defined. At least as far as traditional art historians are concerned, the term is most commonly used when referring to the art of seventeenth-century Italy and Northern Europe and parts of eighteenth-century Central Europe and Latin America.[3] In this respect, it is striking how often seventeenth-century European culture features prominently in Greenaway's films: *The Draughtsman's Contract* is set in an English country house in 1694 and is derived loosely from the conventions of Restoration drama; *Prospero's Books* reworks Shakespeare's *The Tempest* of 1610; *The Baby of Mâcon* tells the story of a French morality play performed in 1659 in the northern Italian court of Cosimo Medici III; the baroque architecture and sculpture of Gian Lorenzo Bernini and other seventeenth-century Roman artists play an important role in *The Belly of an Architect*, as do the paintings of Jan Vermeer in *A Zed & Two Noughts* and those of Frans Hals and other Dutch painters in *The Cook, the Thief, His Wife and Her Lover*; and last but not least, the always powerful scores – whether by Michael Nyman or others – frequently recycle fragments of Purcell and other baroque composers.

Yet it is important to stress that, in spite of his evident fascination with seventeenth-century dialogue, buildings, artefacts and costumes, Greenaway has little interest in making realistic period movies. As he points out in the case of *The Draughtsman's Contract*, the film 'takes cognizance of the 300 years of history that have passed since 1694 and has developed a language based on received opinions of that particular era, preconceived ideas of what that period sounded like. It's also very much aware of twentieth century idioms. I'm reluctant to call it a period movie. I like to think it has great resonances in the twentieth century'.[4] Film critics who detected this self-conscious temporal dou-

FROM ABOVE, L to R
Frames from A Zed & Two Noughts, The Draughtsman's Contract *and* The Cook, the Thief, His Wife and Her Lover

OPPOSITE, FROM ABOVE
A Zed & Two Noughts, *the operating table;* Prospero's Books, *stage-set with books*

bling in such details as the comically exaggerated wigs and the wry business of the living statue were intrigued by the creation of a seventeenth-century world anachronistically governed by what were seen as Wildean conceits, extraordinary cinematic laws, and a decidedly surrealist aesthetic.[5] Reviewing the film in the *New York Times*, Vincent Canby concluded that 'Mr. Greenaway is not Congreve, nor does he pretend to be. *The Draughtsman's Contract* is fun not because it is an imitation of anything, but because its sensibility is that of a 20th-century social satirist'.[6]

Leaving aside for the moment the issue of social satire, we can see that Peter Greenaway's version of the seventeenth century is emphatically postmodern. The past two decades have seen a revival of ornament, pastiche and *trompe l'œil* effects identified with a neo-baroque aesthetic of excess that self-consciously rejects the modernist avant-garde's pursuit of artistic purity. Associated with the rich and famous, with lavish architectural projects, interior design, fashion and exaggerated constructions of femininity, this neo-baroque sensibility is described in Stephen Calloway's recent study, *Baroque Baroque*. Calloway claims that the several minor baroque countercurrents which he charts over the course of the twentieth century culminate, in the 1990s, in a 'Great Baroque Revival'. For him, the baroque is associated with the kind of *grand luxe* embodied in seventeenth-century church decoration and splendid palaces of art. Although the scale of such commissions can seldom be duplicated today, the baroque has come to signify excess in both life and art:

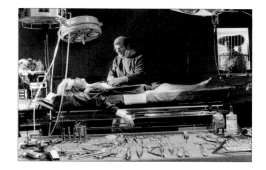

> For 'baroque' is about more than amplitude of form and swirling movement. It is about more than just colour and opulence and the quality of materials or the simple elaboration of decoration. Indeed, 'baroque' has always been far more than just a decorative style; it is ultimately an expression of a certain artistic temperament, an attitude to life and art. The baroque of the twentieth century, this curious, hybrid, referential, highly-strung and self-conscious baroque – this 'Baroque Baroque' – remains our century's one great and whole-hearted affirmation of delight in the richness and grandeur of things.[7]

For many critics, this sort of excess is precisely the hallmark of Peter Greenaway's cinema with its elaborately embellished surfaces containing frames within frames that teem with historical detail, artistic quotation and enigmatic allusion. Add to this a rich play of colour, an exaggerated manipulation of lighting and a larger-than-life soundtrack that flexes its musical muscles in time to the tracking of the camera, and it soon becomes clear that Greenaway is pushing at the limits of film as we have come to accept them. The overall theatrical effect is enhanced by the fact that the action is often staged within framing curtains, before an audience of onlookers who participate to varying degrees in the events portrayed.

The richness of the individual components – the cinematography, the stage sets, the soundtrack, the choreography – owes much to a core of faithful collaborators to whom Greenaway tends to go back for his different projects. Film critic Jonathan Romney foregrounds the collaborative nature of the work when he describes the palace in *Prospero's Books* as a labyrinthine department store: 'The baroque visuals – fashioned as ever by cinematographer Sacha Vierny and designers Jan Roelfs and Ben van Os – are extravagant to the point of profligacy. When a succession of spirits present wedding gifts to the young couple, each gift is only briefly glimpsed, but each is meticulously composed and lit to resemble a Dutch still life.'[8] Roelfs and van Os, who have designed all of Greenaway's films since *A Zed & Two Noughts*, clearly contribute much to the intricately layered look of the finished frame. For instance, they designed the architectural books to function as miniature versions of the larger sets within Prospero's palace: the books lead into the set. Van Os describes how the *Book of Architecture* works: 'You can touch the book, open the book and then you'll see a mirror image of the backside of the book – but it's also the library, so then you go into the library and it's the set. We made the sets just like the pop-up books.'[9]

Another vital element of this richly embellished look is the slow and deliberate cinematography of Sacha Vierny, who has also worked on Greenaway's feature films since *A Zed & Two Noughts*. Greenaway, who had greatly admired Vierny's earlier work, especially in Alain Resnais's *L'Année dernière à Marienbad* (1961) with its lingering shots of the actors framed against sumptuous baroque interiors, showed Resnais's film to the cast and crew of *The Draughtsman's Contract* before filming as an indication of the look he wanted.[10] As Vierny's camera mesmerisingly pans over endless sculptures, gardens, corridors and rooms with gilded mouldings, glass chandeliers and polished floors, the château achieves more of a presence than the actors who wander around it. One understands what Greenaway means when he says of *The Belly of an Architect* that he and Vierny were the 'architects' of the film.[11] The title of honorary architect might also be bestowed on Reinier van Brummelen, lighting designer on many of Greenaway's projects.

Just as vital to the intensely sensuous quality of the films are the distinctive soundtracks provided by composers such as Glenn Branca, Wim Mertens and, most importantly, Michael Nyman who has written the music for many of Greenaway's experimental films and all his features with the exception of *The Belly of An Architect*, *The Baby of Mâcon* and *The Pillow Book*. Nyman's own brand of neo-baroque minimalism, which owes as much to Purcell and Handel as to John Cage and Philip Glass, recycles, forges and plays with musical structures in much the same way that Greenaway juggles images and ideas. Although Nyman often composes the music with only a general knowledge of a particular film's structure, and Greenaway manipulates and rearranges his music during the course of editing, the soundtrack is given a prominence and an independent presence that are unusual in mainstream cinema. In fact, the camerawork is frequently coordinated with the music which, in many instances, determines the rhythm of presentation and prompts the emotional or intellectual response of the viewer. This is particularly evident in the speeded-up music of the decomposition scenes in *A Zed & Two Noughts*, as well as in the film's opening sequence where the credits are coordinated with beats of the music. The soundtrack similarly dominates in the closing moments of *The Cook, the Thief, His Wife and Her Lover* where the characters' movements are orchestrated to a march. At other points the music emphasises the artificiality of film, as in the case of the child singing in an implausibly silenced kitchen, rendering a performance that seems unrelated to the rest of the plot. Like Greenaway's screenplays, Nyman's music is highly self-referential, constantly drawing our attention to its structure by the repetition of rhythmical phrases which gradually vary the themes but also loop back on themselves.[12]

Greenaway clearly chooses his collaborators carefully with a view to enhancing the impact of his films on the senses. Although his personnel varies according to the requirements of individual film scripts – for example, Karine Saporta and Michael Clark were enlisted to choreograph parts of *Prospero's Books* – it is significant that his most frequent collaborators, especially Vierny and Nyman, had already demonstrated an interest in baroque cultural forms before working with Greenaway. The fact that he brings together so many well-established artists from different cultural fields enables him to create a kind of postmodern total artwork which demands that the viewer be familiar with the conventions of different art forms and be able to 'read' the different media. By allowing each art form an unusual degree of autonomy and complexity, and by foregrounding the different arts at various points in a single film, Greenaway constantly challenges his audience's expectations. One is not simply watching an opera or visiting a gallery, but experiencing a complex coordination of different art forms within the compressed duration of a feature film. As Craig Owens pointed out in an influential essay, the impression of confusion and transgression resulting from such mixing of media is itself symptomatic of allegory: 'The allegorical work is synthetic; it crosses aesthetic boundaries. This confusion of genre, anticipated by Duchamp, reappears today in hybridization, in eclectic works which ostentatiously combine previously distinct art mediums.'[13]

Although this mixing of media has characterised all his films since *The Draughtsman's Contract* – which intercuts self-consciously theatrical dialogue with powerfully orchestrated sequences of the draughtsman surveying the grounds of Compton Anstey, close-up details of the manor's paintings and furnishings, and shots of the draughtsman's own drawings in various stages of completion – it reaches unprecedented heights in *Prospero's*

BELOW
Prospero's Books, pop-up books

Books, which comes close to collapsing under the weight of its highly developed constituent elements. On a first viewing, the viewer can scarcely hope to cope adequately with the sheer number and variety of virtuoso performances. The poetry of Shakespeare's text, Gielgud's inimitable voice, Michael Clark's dancing as Caliban, the operatic masque scenes and Nyman's music throughout, the visual displays of bodies, costumes, architecture and scenery, not to mention Greenaway's experimentation with the digital imagery of the Quantel Paintbox which allowed the superimposition of additional frames and layers of dense patterning – all seem to vie chaotically for the viewer's (and the listener's) attention. According to Greenaway, this is what makes his films particularly relevant in an age overloaded with information and audio-visual stimuli: 'The surfaces of my films, from *The Draughtsman's Contract* onwards, are very baroque. They use every device I can think of to indicate the richness and munificence of the world, but always with – and again I'm often accused of this – the central characters behaving in some misanthropic way. If you want to extract some meaning from this, it is that the world is a most magnificent place but people are constantly fucking it up.'[14]

We might, then, expect Stephen Calloway to see in Greenaway's self-consciously excessive cinema a perfect example of his 'Great Baroque Revival', in which he includes such films as Jarman's *Tempest* and *Caravaggio*, Jeunet's *Delicatessen*, Padjanov's *Colour of Pomegranates* and Tim Burton's *Edward Scissorhands*. However, Calloway is curiously reluctant to include Greenaway in this category, though he feels obliged to discuss his work at some length. While he acknowledges Greenaway's use of Nyman's driving neo-baroque music, his seventeenth-century settings, his witty and literate dialogue, his layering of written and spoken words, film and graphic images, and his obsession with themes of lust, decay and death, Calloway concludes: 'In spite of his love of baroque imagery, ultimately Greenaway is not, it seems, a baroque artist at all; in seventeenth-century terms he is not in sympathy with the robust wits of the 1690s, but with the early scientists with their love of taxonomy.'[15] Though an oversimplification of what is at stake in Greenaway's films, this observation points to some of the structural tensions inherent in his work. According to many of the baroque's early theorists, the Dionysian extravagance of baroque cultural forms can be understood only in relation to the Apollonian restraint of classicism.

Since we can scarcely hope to do justice here to the many complex and contradictory accounts of the baroque, it will be more useful to limit our discussion to the art historical work of Heinrich Wölfflin and the theorising of Walter Benjamin, which has recently achieved some prominence in literary and cultural studies. These two critical trajectories seem most likely to shed significant light on Greenaway's own exploration of structural binaries and dialectics, on the one hand, and his use of allegory on the other. As an art student, Greenaway would have encountered the dualisms of an art historical discipline still broadly shaped by its Wölfflinian roots, while as a cultural critic the filmmaker shares many of Benjamin's concerns, including a fascination with the baroque excess characteristic of certain seventeenth and twentieth-century cultural forms. (At this point, we should emphasise that, while we are drawing on both Wölfflin and Benjamin to shed light on Greenaway's experimental use of a baroque idiom, their theoretical perspectives and objects of study remain distinct, just as there are many discrepancies in the way they use ostensibly similar terms; what follows should, then, in no way be construed as an attempt to achieve a synthetic understanding of the baroque.)

Wölfflin inherited the Nietzschean paradigm of a tension between the Apollonian and the Dionysian from his mentor, Jacob Burckhardt, and went on to develop from it a highly influential morphological understanding of the baroque.[16] Seeking to explain how and why styles change, Wölfflin studied the transition from renaissance to baroque through an extensive empirical analysis of hundreds of monuments. Having concluded that there was a fundamental shift from a largely tactile mode of perception in the renaissance to a predominantly visual one in the baroque, he then suggested that this shift could be exhaustively analysed through a set of five binary oppositions mapping the terms of a classical/baroque continuum. The classical pole was identified with the linear, the modelled plane, closed compositions, multiplicity and absolute clarity; the baroque with the painterly, illusionary recession, open compositions, unity and relative clarity.[17]

While such terms have too often become little more than lifeless abstractions used

to identify a period and its monuments, Marshall Brown has argued that Wölfflin intended them to be mobilised in a more complex dialectic which sees irregular and living baroque forms constantly (re)defining themselves in the present against a classical art functioning as a (dead) ideal from the past. Brown's contention that Wölfflin saw the baroque as a fulfilment (or as a kind of Hegelian unfolding) of the classical is based on two facts: first, that when analysing individual works of art, Wölfflin frequently pointed out stylistic confusions between the two poles; second, that for Wölfflin the movement always consisted of a unidirectional flow from classic to baroque. As Brown explains, '[h]istory is always moving toward the baroque and away from the classic. This means that each age serves as the baroque to some earlier classic age and as the classic to a later one'.[18] Thus, Italian classicism comes to represent a scenario of desire and loss that Wölfflin felt the need to revitalise, translate and allegorise from the vantage-point of a German baroque present made manifest, for example, in the sublime and overwhelming emotions of Wagner's music.[19]

As we shall see, Walter Benjamin's thought contains a similar melancholy paralleling of baroque and modern cultural forms, but before we turn down that path it is important to understand how Wölfflin's ideas were taken up and, to a large extent, modified by later scholars. For our purposes, one of the most interesting (and often disparaged) developments was the transformation of Wölfflin's Hegelian unfolding into a reverse pendulum swing from classic to baroque and back again. In art history, this idea engaged a number of writers, including Henri Focillon and Eugenio d'Ors, who rejected traditional notions of periodisation in favour of a cyclical view of change. In his *La Vie des formes*, first published in 1934, Henri Focillon argued that all styles pass through several stages: 1) an early experimental phase of unrest and problem solving; 2) a classical state of stability and achievement; 3) a radiating period of precious refinement; and 4) a baroque state where the art forms proliferate and turn back on themselves, exceeding their own rules and frames, mingling promiscuously with other media, and assuming tortured guises to fit increasingly complex structures of meaning.[20] This conception of the baroque as one phase in an endless cycle of stylistic development that eventually folds in on itself represented a further loosening of the term from its roots in the art of the seventeenth century.[21]

Further detaching the baroque from its historical definition, the Spanish critic Eugenio d'Ors charted some twenty-two different kinds of baroque from pre-history to his own day.[22] Although often dismissed by art historians, d'Ors's ideas were part of a growing popular tendency to divide the history of Western art into periods that were broadly marked by swings from classic to baroque and back again: classical stages included antiquity, the renaissance, neoclassicism and modernism, whereas baroque ones tended to encompass the middle ages, the baroque proper, romanticism and postmodernism. (Of course, these broad periods could be endlessly subdivided to accommodate smaller shifts within them.) Gravity serves as d'Ors's presiding metaphor, enabling him to distinguish between the heaviness of classical forms, governed by centripetal forces, and the tendency of baroque forms, centrifugal in nature, to fly away. Periods are dominated by either classical or baroque principles according to whether the world spirit is in a state of relative *tonicity* (centred, unified, possessing clear contours) or *depression* (dispersed,

Prospero's Books
OPPOSITE
Michael Clark as Caliban
BELOW
Sir John Gielgud as Prospero

multipolar, continuous). D'Ors's key characteristics of the baroque (flight, fugue, multipolarity, dispersion, open systems, centrifugal forces) and the classical (gravity, counterpoint, unipolarity, unity, closed systems, centripetal forces) represent a significant modification of Wölfflin's earlier categories. D'Ors also argued that the arts were governed by a gravitational pull which attracted one art in the direction of another across a continuum; in classical periods the pull was from music to poetry to painting to sculpture to architecture, while in baroque periods the tendency was reversed. Thus, in a classical period, sculpture would tend to become architectural, while in a baroque period architecture would tend towards the sculptural.

D'Ors's privileging of the metaphor of gravity may seem fanciful or overblown, but it has a curious resonance in the world of Peter Greenaway. As we shall see, many of Greenaway's films and curatorial projects explore culture as a site of social and economic conflict in which one system of representation, or set of signifying practices, has to compete with another in terms of their respective 'pull' (and with very real consequences in the world). This is foregrounded in *The Draughtsman's Contract* where Neville's naïve empiricism is no match for the wily allegorising of his aristocratic employers and leads to his violent death. In *The Belly of an Architect*, which deals extensively with the theme of gravity and the tension between centripetal and centrifugal forces, Greenaway revitalises Wölfflin's distinctions between classical and baroque perspectives by manipulating the camera angles and implicating them in a struggle for power and control that plays out in a number of different spheres: artistic, economic, political, sexual, reproductive, physiological. Greenaway describes in one interview how the film's 'consistently centred, static and symmetrical cinematography echoes the sedate and classical mood of the architectural setting' and in another observes that 'the only time when that goes completely awry is the death of Kracklite. Suddenly we see things from the diagonal, we see the whole building from the corner, instead of from the front'. According to the filmmaker, this collapse of symmetry suggests that 'the Apollonian universe that [Kracklite] tried to maintain has been destroyed' and there is nothing left but to allow the laws of gravity to hasten an inevitable death.[23]

The Belly's obsession with gravity is not new to Greenaway's work. Themes of falling and flying play an important role in films like *Windows*, with its catalogue of deaths by defenestration, and *The Falls*, a 186-minute experimental film which wryly documents the symptoms of ninety-two survivors of a Violent Unknown Event (the VUE) that may or may not have been caused by birds and may or may not be causing humans to mutate into birds.[24] The same themes structure an exhibition Greenaway curated for the Louvre in 1992 – *Le Bruit des nuages/Flying Out of This World*.[25] The images he chose from the Louvre's collection for the first two chapters of the exhibition catalogue – 'Earth-bound Gravity' and 'Possibilities of Flight' – constitute a wonderful pictorial commentary on Eugenio d'Ors's morphology of classical and baroque characteristics, though the work of the Spanish critic is not cited. As in the case of *The Falls*, the more allegorical aspects of the Louvre exhibition – particularly chapters six to nine, 'The Stratosphere', 'The Great Fall Begins', 'The Disgraced' and 'Flying in Hell' – remind us that Greenaway's interest in baroque structures is not confined to formal features. Like Walter Benjamin, he is much concerned with how images of death and decay raise fundamental questions concerning the human condition. In this respect, *The Cook, the Thief, His Wife and Her Lover* contains an allegory of loss and redemption, with Georgina and Michael re-enacting biblical scenes of the Fall as they flee naked in a van of rotting meat to escape the wrath of Albert. God is dead, his place taken by a thief.[26]

When Greenaway insists that his cinema is based on allegory, artifice and self-reflexivity, rather than on the conventions of Hollywood realism, he is drawing our attention to the value of allegory as a device of defamiliarisation. Defined by the *OED* as 'speaking otherwise than one seems to speak', allegory is at odds with a sensibility formed by European romanticism with its emotional appeal to personal experience and its aesthetic of lyrical self-expression and unmediated representation. Meaning is neither natural nor spontaneous, says allegory, but depends on conventions that mediate our knowledge both of the world and of ourselves. Greenaway is well aware that a predisposition to allegorical play might make his films seem historically or emotionally distant to many movie goers, who want the film experience to be one of more or less immediate and unproblematic identification with character and situation:

> Allegory is very largely not important to us anymore. We have Father Time with the attribute of the scythe, and maybe Blind Justice holding the scales, but compared to the plethora of allegorical figures that inhabited the seventeenth-century imagination there is no comparison to be made anymore . . . I've often been castigated for not wishing to develop the characters in a three-dimensional sense, but I'm not really interested if the grandmother was called Grace and had a dog called Fido.[27]

But if baroque allegorical structures are unpopular with large sections of the movie-going public, they are currently experiencing a modest but significant revival in the field of cultural theory, where a number of writers have claimed that baroque forms of reasoning can provide important alternatives to the instrumental rationality of modernity.[28] Rather than trying to survey a heteroclite and proliferating corpus of neo-baroque theorising, a more focused approach will lead us to consider Walter Benjamin's (re)turn to (pre-romantic) allegory as an alternative to the symbolism which gained such ascendancy in the eighteenth and nineteenth centuries.[29]

Benjamin deals most fully with the problem of allegory in *The Origin of German Tragic Drama (Ursprung des deutschen Trauerspiels)* which offers a detailed analysis of the often obscure and highly convoluted forms of the much neglected genre of seventeenth-century German tragedy.[30] Attempting (however ambivalently) to rehabilitate a number of long-forgotten playwrights, Benjamin is intrigued by their obsession with allegorical structures, for him a far more characteristic feature of the baroque aesthetic than the morphological traits proposed by Wölfflin. Benjamin's distinction between classical and baroque is based on Friedrich Creuzer's discussion of symbolic and allegorical representation. According to Benjamin, classical works use symbols that tend to be organic, fixed in meaning, self-contained, concentrated and immediately intelligible, while baroque works employ allegories which are inorganic, mobile, frame-breaking, dispersed and situated in the fluidity of time. Allegorical structures hence require more interpretive ingenuity and a sensitive and knowledgeable audience that is willing and able to take pleasure in the active elaboration of discursive meanings from more or less enigmatic fragments.

Benjamin readily acknowledges that the literary critics of his own day tended to disparage German tragedies of the seventeenth century because they objected to the genre's sheer excess: its endless scenes of degradation, cruelty, anguish, violence and death, expressed in a language that was arcane, precious and deliberately archaic. However, Benjamin argues that this assessment is based on an overly literal reading of the genre. Instead of subscribing to the (for him naïve) belief that the playwrights revelled in these things for their own sake, Benjamin argues that such elements should be read allegorically as signs of the inadequacy of knowledge and the misery of the human condition after the expulsion from Paradise. In other words, the emphasis on wretchedness in the profane world deliberately draws attention to the blissful possibilities of redemption, and Benjamin advocates a two-tier critical approach that begins with descriptive commentary but goes on to evaluate the redemptive significance or 'truth value' of cultural artefacts. According to Benjamin, allegorical structures emerge after the Fall, when humans can no longer speak in God's divine language of names (*die Ursprache*). In this post-lapsarian world, knowledge is desperately needed to bridge the gap between thinking and being: since things are separated from their names, meanings do not coincide and languages multiply.

Given this melancholy state of affairs, Benjamin's sympathies lie with the fragmented and tortured forms of baroque art – which draw attention to the human predicament – rather than the organic illusions of classical art which try to obscure it. Nevertheless, the two forms are inextricably related, since the baroque raids classical antiquity for the various elements it recycles: 'The legacy of antiquity constitutes, item for item, the ele-

ments from which the new whole is mixed. Or rather: is constructed. For the perfect vision of this new phenomenon was the ruin. The exuberant subjection of antique elements in a structure which, without uniting them into a single whole, would, in destruction, still be superior to the harmonies of antiquity, is the purpose of the technique which applies itself separately, and ostentatiously, to realia, rhetorical figures and rules.'[31]

As Benjamin points out, the allegorist enjoys enormous power, since, like a sultan or a sadist, s/he creates new meanings by first humiliating and then revitalising the dismembered corpse of classical antiquity. (Later, in his famous essay, 'The Work of Art in the Age of Mechanical Reproduction', he would both celebrate and caution against the use of such cultural recycling by his contemporaries. The fact that new technologies made it possible to remove art from its original context of cult or ritual and reproduce it endlessly in the new exhibitionary order of modern society, thereby destroying its aura, meant that art was at one and the same time more democratically accessible to the masses but also more vulnerable to political manipulation. Hence the call to politicise art as a response to the fascist aestheticisation of politics.)[32] From the outset, Benjamin saw allegorisation as a violent and potentially dangerous process, fraught with the guilt that any pursuit of knowledge necessarily entails. This is especially evident in the *Trauerspiel*, which exhibits an obsessive interest in death, decay, putrefaction and dismemberment: for the body to be used allegorically it must first be ripped apart. If martyrdom 'prepares the body of the living person for emblematic purposes . . . the characters of the *Trauerspiel* die, because it is only thus, as corpses, they can enter into the homeland of allegory. It is not for the sake of immortality that they meet their end, but for the sake of the corpse'.[33]

Like those who found the *Trauerspiel* objectionable, many film critics have been disturbed by Greenaway's use of the human body and have denounced his emotional detachment in dealing with death and decay and bodily functions in general. The last thing they want to see is the rotting flesh of a painter falling from the ceiling, a thief eating the cooked body of his wife's lover, or the corpse of a miracle baby being dismembered by relic seekers. For them, the allegorical use of these and similar raw materials is simply beyond the pale; the human body demands respect and should not be subjected to such indignities, or so the argument goes. In this respect, Greenaway's future plans offer small comfort to the disconcerted. As a worthy successor to the morgue with its drowned bodies in *Death in the Seine* (a film commissioned by a French television channel for the bicentenary of the French Revolution), the rape and dismemberment scenes of *The Baby of Mâcon*, and the flaying of the lover's corpse in *The Pillow Book*, Greenaway has announced the supremely melancholy project of a feature set in the slaughter-fields of the Thirty Years War – the protagonist to be an anatomist searching amongst the corpses for the human soul. In these and other projects, the filmmaker would seem to have located a nerve similar to the one hit by those representatives of the historical avant-garde (of Cubism, Dadaism and early Surrealism) who were still able to offend the public, before such gestures were reduced to a chic radical 'look' by the culture industries.

In his *Theory of the Avant-Garde*, Peter Bürger makes the connection between Benjamin's theory of allegory and the avant-garde's use of montage, which he sees as a phase of allegory. Again the distinction between organic and nonorganic works is paramount:

BELOW
Death in the Seine, *corpses in the water*

OPPOSITE and ABOVE
Frames from Death in the Seine

'Artists who produce an organic work . . . treat their material as something living. For avant-gardistes, on the other hand, material is just that, material. Their activity initially consists in nothing other than in killing the "life" of the material, that is, in tearing it out of its functional context that gives it meaning.'[34] The avant-garde work is thus deliberately and ostentatiously nonorganic in that it makes no attempt to hide the fact that it has been put together from fragments isolated from their original context. As a self-consciously artificial construct, it lays no claim to wholeness but rather allows its constitutive elements a high degree of autonomy (as we have seen in our discussion of the sometimes uneasy coexistence of different art forms in Greenaway's films). This means that any appeal to the hermeneutic circle – the parts to be understood only through the whole, the whole through the parts – is unlikely to meet with satisfaction in 'reading' the allegorical work in Benjamin or Bürger's sense. Allegory, like montage, cannot serve as a guarantee of a work's unity or organic coherence, since it makes no 'assumption of a necessary congruence between the meaning of the individual parts and the meaning of the whole'.[35] In an allegorical work meanings are neither self-evident nor cohesive and tend to offer resistance to totalising interpretations, reminding us that God is, indeed, dead and the world a melancholy place in which all signifying systems are cut adrift: 'All the researches and compositions of the human mind never go beyond the perverse riddles of anagrams, onomatopoeic conceits and the rebus; signification ceases to be a power of logos, and becomes itself immired in the brutishness of things – denotation *non verbis sed rebus*.'[36] Meanings proliferate but cannot be fixed, migrating instead from detail to detail in a play of significations which settle into no hierarchical arrangement, establish no 'truth'.

It is important for us in the 1990s to think seriously about what exactly it means for a contemporary filmmaker to foreground baroque allegorical structures so systematically and so insistently in his films. Is Greenaway attempting to resurrect the avant-garde project with his elaborate collages, or is he simply trading on the recognition factor, sumptuous (re)production values and cultural prestige of some of the finer specimens of Western art and architecture in order to produce a fundamentally conservative art-house cinema? In other words, does his use of cinematic allegory offer the viewer something more than mere nostalgia and the recycling of earlier cultural achievements? (After all, he often claims to be a painter who is working in cinema and trying to modernise a backward medium still largely governed by the conventions of nineteenth-century novels.[37]) Such questions form a thread that will run through our entire discussion of Peter Greenaway's films, exhibitions and installations. At the end of the day, we will try and answer them. In the meantime, let us look first at the way allegory is used centrally in the films to provide a narrative architecture (with special reference here to *The Draughtsman's Contract*) before turning to architecture proper and its allegorical deployment by Greenaway, most extensively in *The Belly of an Architect*.

NOTES

1 Alain Masson, 'Peter Greenaway: La Construction de l'impossible', *Positif* 320, October 1987, p26.

2 Don Ranvaud, 'The Belly of an Architect', *Sight and Sound*, Summer 1987, p196.

3 This is the view advanced by such diverse scholars as Giuliano Briganti (in his introduction to the term in the *Encyclopaedia of World Art*), Anthony Blunt (in *Some Uses and Misuses of the Terms Baroque and Rococo As Applied to Architecture*, British Academy, London, 1973), and Erwin Panofsky (in 'What is Baroque?' in *Three Essays on Style*, [ed] Irving Lavin, MIT Press Cambridge, MA, 1995, pp19-88). There would, however, be some disagreement over the period's most important monuments and chief characteristics.

4 Karen Jaehne, 'The Draughtsman's Contract: An Interview with Peter Greenaway', *Cineaste* 13/2, 1984, p14. In the same interview, Greenaway distances himself from films like Kubrick's *Barry Lyndon*, to which it had been compared.

5 Greenaway himself frequently points to the exaggerated artificiality of the wigs and dialogue, as well as the grass that is too green. The Wildean conceits are noted by Waldemar Januszczak, 'The Draughtsman's Contract', *Studio*, April/May 1983, p21. Pierre Enckell pushes the comparison with the 'poisonous flowers' of English decadence still further by insisting that the film's aesthetic derives above all from Beardsley and *The Yellow Book* ('Les postérités du vice', *L'Avant-Scène Cinéma* 333, October 1984, pp14-15).

6 Vincent Canby, 'The Draughtsman's Contract', *New York Times*, October 3, 1982, p299. He also describes Greenaway as a latter-day surrealist.

7 Stephen Calloway, *Baroque Baroque: The Culture of Excess*, Phaidon Press, London, 1994, p15.

8 Jonathan Romney, 'Prospero's Books', *Sight and Sound*, September 1991, p45.

9 George Dorgan, 'Greenaway's Books of Tricks', *Design*, August 1991, p34.

10 Robert Brown, 'Greenaway's Contract', *Sight and Sound*, Winter 1981/82, p38.

11 Jeremy Clarke, 'Architecture and Mortality', *Films and Filming*, October 1987, p7.

12 Many thanks to Saman Musacchio for his discussions of Nyman's music.

13 Craig Owens, 'The Allegorical Impulse: Toward a Theory of Postmodernism' in *Beyond Recognition: Representation, Power, and Culture* (eds) Scott Bryson, Barbara Kruger, Lynne Tillman, and Jane Weinstock, (intro) Simon Watney, University of California Press, 1992, p58.

14 Brian McFarlene, 'Peter Greenaway', *Cinema Papers* 78, March 1990, p41.

15 Calloway, p232.

16 See Heinrich Wölfflin, *Renaissance and Baroque*, (trans) Kathrin Simon, (intro) Peter Murray, Cornell University Press, Ithaca, 1964. [Original German edition 1888.]

17 These ideas are put forward most systematically in Heinrich Wölfflin, *Principles of Art History*, (trans) MD Hottinger, Dover, New York, 1950. [Original German edition 1922; revised 1929.] Gerald Gillespie has recently suggested that, in the process of importing the term baroque from art history, literary scholars also developed a series of abstract morphological characteristics, including: theatrical, irrational, irregular, tense and dynamic. ('Renaissance, Mannerism, Baroque' in *German Baroque Literature: The European Perspective*, [ed] Gerhardt Hoffmeister, Frederick Ungar Publishing, New York, 1983, p5).

18 Marshall Brown, 'The Classic is Baroque: On the Principle of Wölfflin's Art History', *Critical Inquiry* 9, December 1982, p401.

19 Brown suggests that Wölfflin's idealisation of classicism as irretrievably lost motivated him to write two books entirely devoted to Renaissance art (p394). Citing comments made by Wölfflin in the introduction to *Classic Art*, Brown demonstrates the art historian's essentially tragic view of classical Renaissance art which can only be known in fragmentary, incomplete and reconstituted forms (pp397-98) and situates Wölfflin's sense of loss within a branch of German Romanticism which includes Schiller, Goethe and Humboldt (p398).

20 Henri Focillon, *The Life of Forms in Art*, Zone Books, New York, 1989, pp52-60. [Original French edition 1934.]

21 Tom Conley sees in Focillon's analysis of baroque forms a prototype for Deleuze's study of Leibniz's fold, thereby emphasising its relevance to late twentieth-century thought. See Gilles Deleuze, *The Fold: Leibniz and the Baroque*, (trans) Tom Conley, University of Minnesota Press, Minneapolis, 1993, ppix-xi.

22 Eugenio d'Ors, *Du Baroque*, (trans) Agathe Rouart-Valéry, Gallimard, Paris, 1935. D'Ors is taken to task by both Blunt (p6) and Briganti (p262).

23 The first citation is from Coco Fusco, 'Requiem for an Architect', *Art in America*, February 1988, p35; the second from Clarke, p7; and the third from Marcia Pally, 'Cinema as the Total Art Form: An Interview with Peter Greenaway', *Cineaste* 18/3, 1991, p7.

24 The fact that Greenaway's own father was an amateur ornithologist adds a personal dimension to many allusions in his work, as for example in the subtitle of *A Walk Through H: The Reincarnation of an Ornithologist*.

25 Peter Greenaway, *Le Bruit des nuages/Flying Out of This World*, Réunion des Musées Nationaux, Paris, 1992. Interestingly, Jan Roelfs was involved with the exhibition design.

26 Cf the tongue-in-cheek claims made on the back cover of the published text of *The Falls*, Dis Voir, Paris, 1993: 'We have researched all those VUE victims whose surnames begin with the letters FALL, not being retrospectively unaware of the fact that the FALL has other connotations like the autumn of the world and the Fall of Man.'

27 Marlene Rodgers, 'Prospero's Books – Word and Spectacle: An Interview with Peter Greenaway', *Film Quarterly*, Winter 1991-92, p14.

28 Gilles Deleuze and Michel Serres, for example, both explore the baroque notion of the fold as a philosophical alternative to the tyranny of binary/dialectical thinking. See also Christine Buci-Glucksmann, *Baroque Reason: The Aesthetics of Modernity*, (trans) Patrick Camiller, Sage Publications, London, 1994. [Original French edition 1984.]

29 Nigel Wheale has some useful pages on allegory in his 'Televising Hell: Tom Phillips and Peter Greenaway's TV Dante' in Nigel Wheale (ed), *The Postmodern Arts*, Routledge, London, 1995, pp163-85.

30 Walter Benjamin, *The Origin of German Tragic Drama*, (trans) John Osborne, (intro) George Steiner, NLB, London, 1977.

31 *Ibid* pp178-79.

32 Walter Benjamin, 'The Work of Art in the Age of Mechanical Reproduction' in *Illuminations*, (ed) Hannah Arendt, (trans) Harry Zohn, Schocken Books, New York, 1968, pp217-251.

33 Benjamin, *The Origin of German Tragic Drama*, pp217-18.

34 Peter Bürger, *Theory of the Avant-Garde*, (trans) Michael Shaw, University of Minnesota Press, Minneapolis, 1984, p70.

35 *Ibid* p80.

36 Julian Roberts, 'Melancholy Meanings: Architecture, Postmodernity and Philosophy' in Nigel Wheale (ed), *The Postmodern Arts*, Routledge, London, 1995, p139.

37 For instance, in the interview with Marlene Rodgers (p13) Greenaway complains that cinema has yet to catch up with the conventions of twentieth-century novels.

ON COMMON GROUND
Allegory as Architecture

'Cinema is far too rich and capable a medium to be merely left to the storytellers.'[1] This laconic judgment, by which Greenaway concludes his introduction to the published screen-play of *A Zed & Two Noughts*, sums up both the claims made for cinema and the com-plaints made against it by the filmmaker, particularly during the early part of his career when he was making avant-garde, 'structural' films and, later, at the time of his first forays into the world of feature films in the early eighties. His cinema, we are told, is to be one of analogy and symbol rather than narrative, a cinema of metaphor rather than metonymy. In fact, plot and story are frequently presented as the poor relations of Greenaway's tightly structured films, and he has been a consistently outspoken critic of Hollywood's approach to making movies, which he sees as doing little more than illus-trating nineteenth-century novels.[2]

Such laments recall the terms of the thesis advanced by Claude Lévi-Strauss in his monumental, four-volume study of myth, *Mythologiques*, which first appeared in French between 1964 and 1971 and was a major influence on the structuralist thinking of the late sixties and early seventies. According to Lévi-Strauss, it was towards the end of the sixteenth century that the 'wild thought' (*la pensée sauvage*) of myth – founded on analogy and characterised by a high degree of formal symmetry – started to lose ground rapidly in Europe to the logic of modern science as a way of understanding and ordering the world. Far from disappearing, however, myth would simply be displaced and trans-formed, its formal structures (or architecture) passing into the music of the great ba-roque composers, from Frescobaldi to Bach, while its narrative content would be taken up by the newly emergent and least formalised of all literary genres – the novel. (The frequently noted affinity between architecture and music as arts that do not have imita-tion as their starting point is acknowledged in *Prospero's Books*, where the two are cou-pled in an evocatively titled *Book of Architecture and Other Music*.)

At first sight, Greenaway's cinema would seem to be self-evidently descended from the highly structured music side of the mythological family, rather than the novel branch with its tendency to rambling shapelessness and embarrassing obsession with human psychology and the vicissitudes of history. His films exhibit an architecture which seems to owe less to the unfolding of a coherent narrative than to the demands of visual composition, aleatory sequences, complex language games, taxonomies founded on more or less arbitrary principles of selection – in a word, what Michael Walsh has sweepingly called 'exhaustive rehearsals of the structured materiality of every kind of signifying sys-tem'.[3] As Peter Wollen observes, Greenaway is 'close to movements in modern art and music that employ modular and serial structures. Like many conceptual artists, he is fascinated by lists, grids, catalogues, counting games, and random procedures'. The re-

sult is a resolutely non-naturalistic aesthetic more characteristic of music, one which, 'even in literature and painting . . . subordinates content to formal preoccupations, so that subject matter often seems no more than a pretext. The structure comes first and the content – say, a series of fictions – is then fitted into it, a lesson Greenaway learned from John Cage'.[4] By asking us to think visually and analogically according to patterns which often seem to disrupt the linear flow of the narrative, Greenaway's films consistently undermine our ability and frustrate our desire to read them 'for the story'; we are constantly being asked to look elsewhere to make sense of them.

This challenge to 'look elsewhere' brings to mind a famous passage from Borges and its equally famous commentary by Foucault: 'This passage quotes "a certain Chinese encyclopaedia" in which it is written that "animals are divided into: (a) belonging to the Emperor, (b) embalmed, (c) tame, (d) sucking pigs, (e) sirens, (f) fabulous, (g) stray dogs, (h) included in the present classification, (i) frenzied, (j) innumerable, (k) drawn with a very fine camelhair brush, (l) *et cetera*, (m) having just broken the water pitcher, (n) that from a long way off look like flies." In the wonderment of this taxonomy, the thing we apprehend in one great leap, the thing that, by means of the fable, is demonstrated as the exotic charm of another system of thought, is the limitation of our own, the stark impossibility of thinking *that*.'[5] As Foucault points out, our difficulty with the taxonomy is inseparable from the laughter it provokes, since both stem from the fact that the taxonomy is *heterotopian*, that is, it presupposes for the intelligibility of its categories a common ground that is nowhere apparent. For us to make sense of the taxonomy and the conceptual universe in which it operates, we must discover or construct

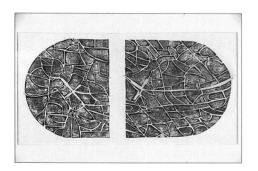
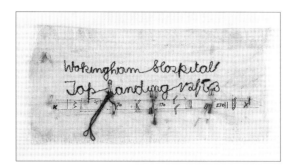
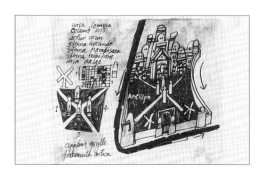

that common ground, we must look elsewhere. In what follows, we shall be suggesting that Greenaway's films explore and dramatise, in a number of different ways, not only this challenge to 'look elsewhere', to find common ground where none is apparent, but also the implications of the failure to do so. It is in this sense that the films can be said both to *use* allegory as a structuring device and to be *about* allegory as a way of making sense of the world.[6]

Allegory, of course, implies narrative, and a cursory glance will tell us that, far from being missing or negligible, narrative is, in fact, almost excessively (or obsessively) present in even the experimental films of the seventies: the solemn inventory of deaths by defenestration in *Windows*; the saga-in-miniature of *Water Wrackets* which owes much to tale-telling à la Tolkien; the mythic journey through the ninety-two painted maps of *A Walk through H*; the riotous collage of narrative fragments in *Dear Phone* – all these films make extensive, if unorthodox, use of narrative. Greenaway's strategy is not to exclude story, but to have it implode upon itself through sheer baroque excess. In this respect, his single most constant inspiration is John Cage's *Indeterminacy* with its ninety (miscounted by Greenaway as ninety-two) one-minute stories of wildly varying word-count, which suggested to the experimental filmmaker 'a way of coping with narrative in the cinema. By overloading a film with thousands of bits of narrative, hundreds of events and millions of characters, you were negating narrative'.[7]

In the same vein, *Vertical Features Remake* is the Borgesian account of bureaucratic attempts to collate, reconstruct and reshape research material pertaining to vertical features in the English landscape left by the legendary Tulse Luper after his death, while *The Falls* is a relentless compilation of ninety-two thumbnail narrative sketches of people variously affected by a Violent Unknown Event (the VUE) and whose names all begin with the letters FALL (from Orchard Falla to Anthior Fallwaste). What is striking about these films, which all use a detached, authoritative voice-over to tell their elaborate stories, is the absence not of plot but of character, in the sense of naturalistic, psychologically motivated representations of individuals played by actors with whom viewers might identify. The feature films will go some way towards remedying this omission, though only incrementally as we shall see in Chapter 3; clearly, for the Greenaway who made *The Draughtsman's Contract* and *A Zed & Two Noughts*, the need for actors was not at all self-evident and their full potential by no means a given. (In an interview published to coincide with the release of *The Draughtsman's Contract* in France, Michel Ciment suggests that Neville's experience as a draughtsman is an apt metaphor for Greenaway's history as a filmmaker, since despite Neville's efforts to keep human beings out of the picture, they keep spilling into the frame and leaving their messy traces.[8] After this initial breakthrough, the representation of human bodies, both naked and clothed, will play an increasingly important role in Greenaway's features and television work.)

If the films appear to subordinate the demands and expectations of realist narrative to other (often very intricate) forms of ordering, it is nevertheless true that plotting, in all senses of the term, is an essential, if allegorical, activity in Greenaway's world. In *Reading for the Plot: Design and Intention in Narrative*, Peter Brooks proposes four senses of the word 'plot', drawn from the *American Heritage Dictionary*:

1 (a) a small piece of ground, generally used for a specific purpose

   (b) a measured area of land; lot

2 a ground plan, as for a building; chart; diagram

3 the series of events consisting of an outline of the action of a narrative or drama

4 a secret plan to accomplish a hostile or illegal purpose; scheme.[9]

He then goes on to uncover the 'subterranean logic' (or common ground) that might be seen to connect these apparently heterogeneous meanings:

Common to the original sense of the word is the idea of boundedness, demarcation, the drawing of lines to mark off and order. This easily extends to the chart or diagram of the demarcated area, which in turn modulates to the outline of the literary work. From the organised space, plot becomes the organising line, demarcating and diagramming that which was previously undifferentiated. We might think here of the geometrical expression, plotting points, or curves, on a graph by means of coordinates, as a way of locating something, perhaps oneself. The fourth sense

BELOW
Vertical Features Remake – The Research,
mixed media on paper, 1974

OPPOSITE
The Falls: *(above)* The Bird on the Hill, *ink on paper, 1978, (below)* collage, 1980

of the word, the scheme or conspiracy, seems to have come into English through the contaminating influence of the French *complot*, and became widely known at the time of the Gunpowder Plot.[10]

If we have quoted this passage at length, it is because it resonates in surprising ways with Greenaway's own approach to narrative and, more particularly, offers a number of intriguing insights into the plotting of *The Draughtsman's Contract*, which we shall attempt to 'read' as a case study of his more general allegorising tendencies.[11]

The action takes place in August 1694. Mr Neville, the draughtsman of the title, is persuaded by Mrs Herbert and her daughter, Sarah Talmann,[12] to execute a series of twelve drawings of Compton Anstey, Mr Herbert's much-cherished country house. (The property has come to him by marriage, and he has no son.) The drawings, which are to be done over a period of twelve days during Mr Herbert's absence in Southampton, are to be presented by Mrs Herbert to her husband on his return in the hope of effecting a reconciliation between man and wife and thereby saving an ailing marriage. The function (or meaning) of the drawings is thus twofold: 1) they are to *represent* Mr Herbert's property and hence his social standing, his *estate*; 2) they are to *symbolise*, through their status as *gift*, the conjugal relationship with their commissioner. But the contract drawn up between Neville and Mrs Herbert violates the spirit of both these intended meanings in so far as, in addition to a fee of eight guineas per drawing, it gives the arrogant young draughtsman free access not only to the good lady's home and table, but also her body, which, we are reminded, is also a part (though not a highly valued part, coming somewhere after house, garden and horse) of her husband's property.[13] In the next few days we see Neville striding about that property, emptying the landscape of people and transferring the various 'views' of Compton Anstey, graphically framed by his viewfinder, onto his conscientiously squared-off paper. For this literal recorder of 'what is there', nothing will be added and nothing left out: what you see is what you get. At the same time we see Neville at play, equally businesslike, equally arrogant, exacting his pleasure in a series of joyless couplings that leave Mrs Herbert in a state of evident physical and emotional distress.

On the sixth day of the contract, with the sixth drawing well on the way to completion, a second contract is initiated, this time by Mrs Talmann who points out to the draughtsman that the first half-dozen drawings all contain items of Mr Herbert's clothing, which seem to have been strewn randomly about the property:

Mrs Talmann: That shirt, Mr Neville, is prominent enough in your drawing. Would it be possible, do you think, to disguise its presence?

Mr Neville: Madame, I try very hard never to distort or to dissemble.

Mrs Talmann: Would that always be your method of working, Mr Neville?

Mr Neville: It would.

Mrs Talmann: Well, let me make a little speech. In your drawing of the north side of the house, my father's cloak lies wrapped around the feet of a figure of Bacchus. In the drawing of the prospect over which my husband turns an appreciative gaze, you will have noticed that there is unclaimed a pair of riding boots. In the drawing of the park from the east side, it is possible to see leaning against my father's wardroom a ladder usually put to use for the collecting of apples. And in the drawing of

The Draughtsman's Contract

FROM ABOVE
*The drawing with items of Mr
Herbert's clothing; Neville with
his viewfinder*

the laundry, there is a jacket of my father's slit across the chest. Do you not think
that before long you might find the body that inhabited all those clothes?

The enigmatic implication of Mrs Talmann's 'little speech' is that the absent body is now
a corpse and that the drawings might somehow be read as evidence of foul play, evidence which might be used to frame the draughtsman just as he has framed the views.
When Neville protests the items are innocent, Sarah responds that 'taken one by one
they could be so construed', but that taken together they call for 'a connecting plot', 'an
interpretive plot' that could be used to account for her father's disappearance. As an
'accessory to misadventure', the draughtsman is in need of protection, and this Mrs
Talmann will provide in exchange for *her* use of *his* body at her pleasure. A second
contract is thus drawn up which mirrors the first, and the last six drawings will bear the
metonymic traces, not of Mr Herbert's missing body, but of Sarah Talmann's adultery
with 'a paid servant' of her mother's.

Shortly after this conversation about 'connecting plots' and their possible implications,
a second exchange takes place on a similar subject, this time between Neville and Mrs
Herbert. Neville has taken a painting down from the wall – it is Januarius Zick's allegorical *Homage to Isaac Newton*, anachronistically present in 1694 – and roughly interrogates Mrs Herbert about her husband's 'eccentric and eclectic taste' as a collector: perhaps he has 'an eye for optical theory' or an 'interest in the pictorial conceit'? It is Mrs
Herbert's turn to play the innocent, responding indifferently that the fact that it represents a garden is probably explanation enough for her husband's acquisition of the picture. Neville persists: 'Do you see, Madam, a narrative in these apparently unrelated
episodes? There is drama, is there not, in this overpopulated garden. What intrigue is
here? . . . What infidelities are portrayed here? Do you think that murder is being pre-
pared?' Neville has known from the start that, as an artist, he enjoys a certain power: 'I
hold the delight or despondency of a man of property by putting his house in shadow
or in sunlight. Even possibly I have control over the jealousy or satisfaction of a husband
by depicting his wife, Sir, dressed or undressed.'[14] Now he has learned that the circulation of power is a more complicated business than he had thought, that the meaning of
a painting or drawing shifts according to the codes invoked, and that the possession of
those codes constitutes a cultural capital capable of reinforcing or unsettling social hier-
archies. Power (and property) can be celebrated, derided, or even, if one is fortunate
enough to have the help of an attractive woman, usurped. But the stakes are high, and
for the would-be usurper the price of failure is death.

With the drawings finished – 'looking at them is akin to pursuing a complicated allegory', observes Mr Seymour – and Neville preparing to take his leave, the body of Mr
Herbert is found in the moat. (Like so many of Greenaway's male characters, he apparently could not swim.) Neville's departure is followed by a round of frantic plotting and
counter-plotting, a veritable feeding frenzy of insider trading, as various characters vie
for possession (and for different 'readings') of the drawings. In the blackmarket free-for-
all that ensues, Mrs Herbert finds herself pitted against Mr Noyes, the estate manager to
whom she had previously been engaged and who had drawn up and witnessed both
contracts; as a man of talent but no property, he is ready to use the drawings (and the
contracts) in any way he can, either to protect himself or to incriminate others. Mrs

Talmann, in turn, must deal with her husband, a German Protestant whose impotence endangers the line of succession and who has been made aware by Noyes of the story of his wife's adultery told in the last six drawings. When Neville returns a week later to make a thirteenth drawing of the house (a view of the statue of the riderless horse next to the moat where Mr Herbert's body had been discovered), he will once more enjoy Mrs Herbert's favours, this time apparently with her free consent, and will learn from Sarah Talmann that she herself has used him, less for her pleasure, than to produce an heir. That night he is confronted, as he sits by torchlight in front of his unfinished thirteenth drawing, by Noyes, Talmann and other members of their circle who close ranks to rid the community (a microcosm of England's ruling class of landed gentry) of an outsider who threatens to become a nuisance. Before beating him to death and burning his drawings, they ritually put out his eyes with a flaming torch.

The film's 'plot' thus revolves around two contracts, which enjoy an unusual legal status in that each constitutes a transgression of a previous contract – that of marriage; by specifying the terms and conditions of adultery, by legislating infidelity, each contract implicitly legitimates an illicit act. Furthermore, by contracting for sex within an exchange of goods and services, by reducing the body (or person) of, first, Mrs Herbert, then Mr Neville, to pieces of property or merchandise in a circuit of exchange, the two contracts simply parody a more general political economy that makes a wife the property of her husband and subjects the artist to his patrons' desires. In the terms already quoted from Peter Brooks's discussion of 'plot', the contracts can be seen as functioning analogously to the drawings they commission and control, in so far as both involve 'the drawing of lines to mark off and order' and the 'plotting' of both physical and social space. This is reflected in the scenes of Neville at work with the tools of his trade (viewfinder and squared-off paper), in the restrictive 'curriculum' that regulates the movement of people in the landscape while the drawings are being made, and in the constrained geometry of bodies in various sexual postures that flows indirectly from the dispositions of the contracts. More than simply delivering what has been contracted, both the drawings and the sex 'scenes' become the physical *embodiment* of contractual law itself, the double inscription of that which legislates 'the drawing of lines to mark off and order' and makes possible the 'plotting' of both Compton Anstey and Mrs Herbert's body.[15]

What of the other kind of 'plotting', the fourth dictionary sense of the word, the scheme or conspiracy? Plots of this kind abound in Greenaway's films, from the various theories concerning the 'responsibility of birds' hinted at in *The Falls* to the water-tower conspirators of *Drowning by Numbers*. In modern literature, Brooks reminds us, 'the organizing line of plot is more often than not some scheme or machination, a concerted plan for the accomplishment of some purpose which goes against the ostensible and dominant legalities of the fictional world, the realization of a blocked and resisted desire. Plots are not simply organizing structures, they are also intentional structures, goal-oriented and forward-moving'.[16] Here again, *The Draughtsman's Contract* treats 'plot' not simply as a narrative engine that moves the story forward but as an elaborate metaphor or conceit that thematises 'plotting' in terms of a political allegory of patrimonial succession. For while the first contract provides in a fairly straightforward way for Mrs Herbert's 'plot' of marital reconciliation and Neville's 'plot' of seduction and social climbing, the second complicates matters considerably. For one thing, it displaces and disrupts the first two plots by reading into the first six drawings the traces of a conspiracy, interpreting the figured absence of Mr Herbert's body and transforming the 'plotted' space of Compton Anstey into a scene of murder and intrigue. Then, through Mrs Talmann's scheme to provide an heir to the property her father had married into, it delineates a 'plot' (figured in the traces of adultery that appear in the last six drawings) of succession and usurpation that plays out in miniature – through a whole range of motifs and emblems that function both analeptically and proleptically – the contemporary political and sectarian history of England (and its 'oldest colonies', Scotland and Ireland) in the transition from the Catholic convert James II to the Protestant William III of Orange.

The most obvious example of this kind of allusion is the sustained allegorical motif of fruit of all kinds, most prominently plums, apples, limes, oranges, pineapples and pomegranates. Horticultural conceits – of planting, grafting, pruning and bearing fruit – abound and their allegorical application to the human spheres of sexuality, procreation and political history is not allowed to go unremarked.[17] ('The English are not blessed with the most appropriate fecundity at the moment', comments Talmann. 'They can raise colonies but not heirs to the throne.') A more subtle, proleptic allusion is to the mole – the famous 'little gentleman in the black velvet jacket' of the Jacobite toasts – that will unwittingly unhorse William III in 1702, some eight years after the events portrayed in *The Draughtsman's Contract*. Mrs Herbert's gardener says that moles are to be encouraged for good luck and the destruction of one's enemies; Neville replies that they trip up horses, thereby making an anachronistic connection – for our benefit, not Mrs Herbert's – between Mr Herbert, whose horse has just returned lame and riderless, and the king who will later die of pneumonia following his fall.

It is against this background of historical allegory that Michael Walsh can argue that 'the dramatic motor of the film is a crisis in symbolic paternity, expressed most obviously as the departure, disappearance, and death of Mr. Herbert'.[18] Walsh offers a Lacanian reading of this crisis as a failure to properly locate the Name of the Father and links this failure, on the one hand, with psychosis (or paranoia), in which the paternal signifier is missing from the Symbolic, and on the other, with mourning, in which a swarm of images seeks to repair the damage caused by its absence from the Real. In *The Draughtsman's Contract*, the figure of the missing father generates 'a paranoid, conspiratorial maze that suspends cognitive surety' as we, along with Neville, are led up a garden path strewn with red herrings and empty signifiers, inextricably enmeshed in a discursive net of double meanings, significant pauses and veiled allusions.

As Walsh notes, the swarm of images that seek to stand in for the missing Mr Herbert are literalised in Neville's drawings, most especially the one in which the usurper Talmann's body is represented against the background of the landscape with the face left blank until the appropriate likeness can be filled in. In art historical terms, Simon Watney reminds us that '[t]he position of the viewing figure in the landscape is thus crucial, since the garden was expressly designed as an emblematic equivalent to his or her social standing. The emblematic garden, with its statues and inscriptions, its symbolic plants and its allegorical geometry of vistas and flower-beds, offered itself as a confirmation of the "right" to possession, a narrative of many-levelled connotations to be explored and

The Draughtsman's Contract

OPPOSITE
Drawing of Mr Talmann with landscape

LEFT
Neville drawing Mr Talmann

deciphered at one's leisure. It was thus regarded as a kind of proposition in its own right, and as a model for social relations as a whole'.[19] In this sense, we might see Neville's drawings as themselves figuring a contract, or deed of property, with the name of the titular owner left blank. We would therefore suggest that, while Walsh's reading of the film is an intrinsically interesting and productive one, it is even more helpful for our understanding of the allegory to foreground the fact that this 'crisis in symbolic paternity' is above all a crisis in legitimacy and authority. Instead of asking, *Who (or where) is the Father?*, the central questions (in a historical context marked by the memory of revolution, regicide, usurpation and constitutional reform) then become: *To whom does Compton Anstey (read: England) legitimately belong?* and *Who has the authority to decide such matters?* This slight change of emphasis not only helps to clarify what is at stake historically (both in 1694, under William of Orange, and in 1982 in Thatcher's Britain[20]) but will also be useful when we return to examine other aspects of the allegory developed in *The Draughtsman's Contract*.

Clearly, stories of problematic or disrupted succession play an important part in the history of narrative structures. Interestingly for us, Peter Brooks takes as his paradigmatic case of hermeneutic plotting Arthur Conan Doyle's *The Musgrave Ritual*, a Sherlock Holmes story that he reads as an 'allegory of plot' in which the detective, confronted with a series of apparently unrelated enigmas, seeks to discover the 'chain of events' that will link them, 'to devise some common thread upon which they might all hang'.[21] This he finds in the ritual itself, an apparently meaningless text passed on in the Musgrave family from father to son and signifying nothing more (to them) than an affirmation of the continuity of their line. Holmes's insight is that the ritual is to be 'read' as a set of directions for plotting points, which he proceeds to follow by pacing out distances in the grounds of the Musgraves' country house. His 'plotting' leads him to the 'buried treasure', the sadly deteriorated remains of the lost crown of the Stuarts, symbol of a more momentous, historical transmission in which male members of the Musgrave family had once been implicated.

For Brooks, the important lesson to be learned from Conan Doyle's story as an allegory of plot is that 'the incomprehensible metaphor of transmission must be unpacked as a metonymy, literally by plotting its cryptic indications out on the lawn. Narrative is this acting out of the implications of metaphor . . . [T]he terminal points of the narrative offer a blinded metaphor of transmission (the ritual as "absurd business") and an enlightened metaphor of transmission (the ritual as part of the history of English monarchy)'.[22] Both metaphors – the 'enigma' of the missing body of the Father/King, the 'evidence' of the making of an heir – are centrally present in *The Draughtsman's Contract*. In the film, however, their narrative unpacking, as 'plotted' from drawing to drawing, functions more ironically (and more cynically) than in the classic detective story, the allegorical passage from blindness to enlightenment being followed by an epilogue that brings literal blindness and death – Neville's punishment for having successfully, but too late, unpacked the metaphor he has unwittingly helped to 'plot'.

It is interesting to note that Neville's initial transition, at the prompting of Sarah Talmann, from recording to 'reading', recalls the scene in Antonioni's *Blow-Up* in which the young photographer attempts to reconstruct, through a series of enlargements, the chain of sinister events he has innocently recorded in the photographs he has taken in a London park. By another telling coincidence, Peter Brooks chooses this retrospective transformation of image into story as an example of one of those 'moments where we seize the active work of structuring revealed or dramatized in the text . . . [F]inding, or inventing, the plot that seems to lie hidden in the shadows of the park and in the grainy darkness of the photographs could alone give meaning to the events, which, while recorded through the veracious and revealing "objective" lens of the camera, remain unavailable to interpretation so long as they are not plotted'.[23] Kracklite, in *The Belly of an Architect*, will provide a paranoid variation on this theme with his series of enlarged photocopies of images of the Emperor Augustus's belly, on which he tries to draw, quite literally, an allegory of his own poisoning at the hands of his wife.

Have we by now exhausted the complexities of 'plot' in *The Draughtsman's Contract*? Not quite, for the film's narrative structure embodies yet another allegory, this time of vision – the 'plot' of contemporary art history. When Neville claims that he draws only what he sees, without distorting or dissembling, that he records what is before him without allegorical intent, he is (somewhat disingenuously, it is true) situating his own practice in relation to the fundamental art historical dichotomy of his age. Svetlana Alpers has distinguished in this respect between 'textual' and 'visual' cultures as realised, respectively and schematically, in the narrative and allegorical art of the Italian Renaissance with its weight of classical erudition and conventionally encoded knowledge, and the descriptive art of the seventeenth-century Dutch masters, with its emphasis on 'seeing' the world empirically for what it is, without the 'prior frame' of interpretive plot or cultural allusion. According to this view, Greenaway's film would be set at the crossroads between an old art of 'reading' and a new art of 'seeing', an art in which the eye becomes 'a central means of self-representation and visual experience a central mode of self-consciousness'.[24]

In terms made familiar by Foucault in *The Order of Things*, we are witness to a conflict between the investments held in the established Renaissance tradition of interpretation through resemblance (or analogy) and those being placed in a new order based, not on drawing things together, but on keeping them apart (or discriminating).[25] In this sense, as we have seen, Neville's twelve discrete drawings are brought under control and made available for manipulation by the Whig landowners (historically the ruling class of English capitalism) through a process of 'drawing together', of providing a 'connecting plot' or 'common thread'. We have been told at the beginning of the film that those gathered under the Herberts' roof 'own a fair slice of England'; in the struggle for power that follows Mr Herbert's death, Neville, who, like the courtesan Mrs Pierpoint, is 'strictly not of the company but a part of its property', will attempt through his contracts with Mrs Herbert and Mrs Talmann to become a player in their game. Unfortunately for him, despite his arrogance and his ambition, he does not quite grasp the rules and is no match for his aristocratic adversaries. His 'art of the eye' has its analogue in his relative innocence of the ways of their world (where, precisely, there is 'more than meets the eye') and the price that will be exacted for consistently 'misreading' what he has 'seen' will be blindness and death.[26]

Neville's exemplary failure brings us to the last level of allegory in *The Draughtsman's*

Contract, one that maps the art historical onto the historico-political. John Berger posed the key question – that of legitimacy and authority in the transmission of a society's cultural legacy – more than twenty years ago, but it still has resonance today though its language is no longer in fashion: 'The idea of innocence faces two ways. By refusing to enter a conspiracy, one remains innocent of that conspiracy. But to remain innocent may also be to remain ignorant. The issue is not between innocence and knowledge (or between the natural and the cultural) but between a total approach to art which attempts to relate it to every aspect of experience and the esoteric approach of a few specialised experts who are the clerks of the nostalgia of a ruling class in decline. (In decline, not before the proletariat, but before the new power of the corporation and the state.) The real question is: to whom does the meaning of the art of the past properly belong? To those who can apply it to their own lives, or to a cultural hierarchy of relic specialists?'[27] In this respect, we should note that Scott Malcomson has argued that Neville's relationship to the aristocracy (including his punishment for being a 'bad reader') is analogous to our own mystification as viewers at the hands of an all-powerful author, Peter Greenaway, who controls and manipulates our reactions as (necessarily) imperfect readers of culture.[28] According to this reading, there would be a perfect isomorphism between Neville's represented plight and our own implication in representational structures which function in reality as structures of repression, as a kind of cultural straitjacket applied to control our delusions of equality. (In Foucault's terms, the film would be a parable of discipline and punishment directed against us, the audience.) We will return to this question in our last chapter, where we discuss the reception of Greenaway's work in the context of a more general examination of how the struggle for possession and control of the past is played out in the moves of today's culture industry.

For the moment, it is sufficient to note that Greenaway's films are marked by an insistent anxiety over control of the artistic product. Neville and his drawings, Kracklite and his exhibition – these are the two most obvious cases of artists who lose control of their projects. We shall look more closely at Kracklite's problems in the next chapter, but it is worth pointing out here that Neville and he are not simply 'artist figures' playing out the central role in their respective 'artist films';[29] they are both stand-ins for the filmmaker, an analogy which is more highly developed in *The Belly of an Architect* where the problems surrounding the organisation of an international art exhibition offer more scope for parallels with Greenaway's own artistic practice. In *The Draughtsman's Contract*, the analogy is less sustained, though perhaps more immediately visual. Svetlana Alpers has argued that the emergence of a visual culture based on empirical observation in seventeenth-century Holland was made possible by a new-found trust in optical devices such as the camera obscura, the microscope and lenses in general.[30] Thus, Robert Hooke's 1694 report to the Royal Society, 'An instrument of Use to take the Draught, or Picture of a Thing', promotes the use of the camera obscura to produce truthful drawings of foreign places to counter the false images of travel narratives.[31]

In this respect, Neville's viewfinder, present in so many shots, is an extraordinarily interesting piece of property with an elusive life of its own. In the first instance, on the level of Neville's own conception of his practice as a draughtsman, it acts as an indication of the same kind of trust in optical devices that we see in Hooke's Royal Society report or in seventeenth-century Dutch painting. On another level, that for example of Mrs Talmann's 'little speech' with its call for a 'connecting plot', it is at least in part recuperated from the empirical world of 'seeing' and made available for service in the constructed world of 'knowing' and 'reading', where it can be assimilated to something approximating Alberti's 'prior frame' of allegorical painting.[32] Most importantly, however, the viewfinder functions as the very emblem of the filmmaker in the film, making us aware that we are dealing with three distinct levels of representation. In fact, the device of the viewfinder, like the use of the drawings themselves and their implication in an allegorical plot, has the double effect of making us look much harder at what is represented and of imposing a self-reflexive awareness of our own implication in the process of looking.

As we, the audience, look through Neville's device, do we see what he sees (a purely hypothetical 'degree zero' landscape devoid of allegorical meaning), what Sarah Talmann wants him to see (a framed allegory which *she* authors and controls), what Greenaway (perhaps) wants us to see (an allegory of a higher logical type which *represents* the dialectic between the first two levels and which *he* authors and controls), or something quite different again? In terms of Foucault's analysis of a modern society founded on techniques of surveillance, we might see in the first use of the viewfinder an attempt to discipline the landscape (by emptying it of the propertied class it allegorises), in the second an attempt to discipline the upstart Neville (by the reinscription of an allegory which escapes him), and in the third an attempt to discipline and/or liberate us as viewers (by making us aware of the inadequacies of the first two 'readings'). As Greenaway explains, while the draughtsman's viewfinder is loosely modelled on ones used by Canaletto and Dürer, it has been 'made into more of an optical device, a sort of early piece of astrological, astronomical material. But again it's a question that when a cameraman looks down a viewfinder, that is the grid he sees as well. So in a sense the film is about what the cameraman sees, what the draughtsman sees and what we as an audience see, and the representational difference between the three'.[33] And it is Mr Talmann who, as a good European, shall have the last (parodic) word on the matter. 'To be an English painter', he tells Neville, 'is a contradictory term' — thereby anticipating by almost three hundred years Truffaut's (in)famous wisecrack about the words *English* and *cinema* being incompatible.[34]

NOTES

1 Peter Greenaway, *A Zed & Two Noughts*, Faber and Faber, London, 1986, p15.

2 See, for example, Gavin Smith, 'Food for Thought: Peter Greenaway Interviewed', *Film Comment* 26/3, 1990, pp55, 58-59.

3 Michael Walsh, 'Allegories of Thatcherism: The Films of Peter Greenaway' in Lester Friedman, (ed), *Fires Were Started: British Cinema and Thatcherism*, University of Minnesota Press, Minneapolis, 1993, p257.

4 Peter Wollen, 'The Last New Wave: Modernism in the British Films of the Thatcher Era' in Lester Friedman (ed), *Fires Were Started: British Cinema and Thatcherism*, University of Minnesota Press, Minneapolis, 1993, p47.

5 Michel Foucault, *The Order of Things: An Archaeology of the Human Sciences*, trans Alan Sheridan, Tavistock Publications, London, 1970, pxv. Greenaway is quoted in an issue of *BFI News* 46 (January 1981), p3, as being 'fascinated by documentation, catalogues, classifications, lists of objects, encyclopaedias (what could be more arbitrary than the arrangement of heterogeneous objects under the same letter of the alphabet as in a dictionary)'.

6 Simon Watney makes the same point when he writes that '*The Draughtsman's Contract* is fundamentally and essentially an allegory. And more than that, it is a film *about* allegory' ('Gardens of Speculation: Landscape in *The Draughtsman's Contract*' in Philip Hayward [ed], *Picture This: Media Representations of Visual Art and Artists*, John Libbey, London and Paris, 1988, p183). But he goes on to say that 'the actual plot, as such, will not concern [him]' (*ibid* p184). As we shall attempt to show, allegory and plot are, in *The Draughtsman's Contract*, inseparable.

7 Interview in *Stills* 6 (May-June 1983), p63. Greenaway would seem to share Lyotard's mistrust of metanarratives, those teleological tales which societies tell themselves to provide a sense of destiny and ordered progression. This is most evident in *A Zed & Two Noughts*, where the 'dreary fiction' of Darwinism is no more helpful than Genesis in helping the Deuce brothers come to terms with mortality in general and the death of their wives in particular.

8 Michel Ciment, 'Entretien avec Peter Greenaway', *Positif* 276 (February 1984), p5.

9 Peter Brooks, *Reading for the Plot: Design and Intention in Narrative*, Vintage Books, New York, 1985, pp11-12. This part of our study develops and expands on a discussion started in Bridget Elliott and Anthony Purdy, 'Artificial Eye/Artificial You: Getting Greenaway or Mything the Point?' in: Anthony Purdy (ed), *Literature and the Body*, Rodopi, Amsterdam, 1992, pp179-211.

10 Brooks, p12.

11 To date, the script of *The Draughtsman's Contract* has not been made available in book form. However, a bilingual script (French/English) was published in *L'Avant-Scène Cinéma* 333 (October 1984), pp46-117.

12 Is it one of Greenaway's many red herrings or merely a curious coincidence that Talman (with only one *n*) was the name of one of the leading baroque architects of the day? William Talman (1650-1759) was Comptroller of King's Works from 1689 to 1702 and built a number of the most famous and architecturally influential country houses of the period. He was born in Wiltshire, the supposed setting for Compton Anstey.

13 On the Restoration's tendency to reduce 'men and women to physical, bargainable carriers of estates and incomes', see Raymond Williams, *The Country and the City*, Paladin, London, 1975, p69.

14 Two kinds of contemporary painting are brought to mind by Neville's comments: the first would depict a 'man of property' standing in the foreground with his house and estate in the background, as in Hendrick Danckerts's *Rose, the Royal Gardener, Presenting Charles II with the First Pineapple Grown in England*, a painting to which *The Draughtsman's Contract* alludes implicitly through its fruit symbolism; the second would represent the 'man of property''s mistress, portrayed naked as in Lely's portrait of Nell Gwynne commissioned by Charles II.

15 The word *contract* has clear and important echoes in the period. John Locke's *Two Treatises of Government*, which set forth his social contract theory, were published in 1690, a year after his return to England in the wake of William of Orange. The same year saw publication of his *Essay concerning Human Understanding*, the first major empiricist theory of knowledge. Both works are relevant to our discussion of the film's allegorical import.

16 Brooks, p12.

17 Vernon Gras sees the figure of the earth goddess, representing the seasonal cycle of death and rebirth and figured in *The Draughtsman's Contract* by the pomegranate associated with the Demeter-Persephone myth, as central to all Greenaway's work. See Vernon Gras, 'Dramatizing the Failure to Jump the Culture/Nature Gap: The Films of Peter Greenaway', *New Literary History* 26 (1995), pp123-43. On this count, Greenaway's gender politics, often refreshingly egalitarian when it comes to the representation of bodies, seem mired in an unfortunate essentialism.

18 Walsh, p262.

19 Watney, p187.

20 Walsh sees in Greenaway 'an allegorist whose features comment indirectly but decisively on the crisis of postimperial Britain to which Thatcherism also responds' and makes the point that his two most successful films with audiences, *The Draughtsman's Contract* and *The Cook, the Thief, His Wife and Her Lover*, mark the beginning and the end of the Thatcher period: 'These two films also parenthesize the entire history of the oldest continuously existing bourgeois state in the world, covering the ground from its establishment in the Glorious Revolution of 1688 to the present' (Walsh, p260).

21 Brooks, p24.

22 *Ibid* pp26-27.

23 *Ibid* p35.

24 Svetlana Alpers, *The Art of Describing: Dutch Art in the Seventeenth Century*, University of Chicago Press, 1983, pxxv. On the parallel evolution of the garden itself, from the emblematic, enclosed, formal gardens of the Restoration in which could be 'read' many things (including certain inscriptions of privilege and power) to the 'natural' look of the landscaped gardens of the eighteenth century, see Watney, pp187-90.

25 Foucault, p55. For Watney, too, Foucault's study is a key frame of reference for a 'reading' of *The Draughtsman's Contract*, as the terms of his analysis make clear: 'Set in a period which still conceived its world in allegorical terms, prior to the encroachments of rationalist or positivist thought, it is a film which encourages modern audiences to reflect on the profound changes in the history of European representation over the last three centuries, and their consequences for how we think ourselves and the world we share' (Watney, p183). He goes on to make the interesting point that the film's 'range of intertextual reference is not so much with other films as with other modes of representation, with theories of representation itself' (*ibid* p184).

26 It is perhaps worth recalling Paul de Man's claim that '[a]llegorical narratives tell the story of the failure to read [. . .] Allegories are always allegories of metaphor and, as such, they are always allegories of the impossibility of reading' (*Allegories of Reading,* Yale University Press, 1979, p205).

27 John Berger, *Ways of Seeing*, BBC and Penguin Books, 1972, p32.

28 Scott Malcomson, 'The Draughtsman's Contract', *Film Quarterly* (Winter 1983-84), pp34-40.

29 John Walker's *Art and Artists on Screen*, Manchester University Press, 1993, has useful chapters on *The Draughtsman's Contract* and *The Belly of an Architect* as artist films and makes a good starting point for anyone wanting to read about the representation of art and artists in cinema.

30 Alpers, pp32-33.

31 *Ibid* p74.

32 Cf. Alpers, pxix: 'In referring to the notion of art in the Italian Renaissance, I have in mind the Albertian definition of the picture: a framed surface or pane situated at a certain distance from a viewer who looks through it at a second or substitute world. In the Renaissance this world was a

stage on which human figures performed significant actions based on the texts of the poets. It is a narrative art. And the ubiquitous doctrine *ut pictura poesis* was invoked in order to explain and legitimize images through their relationship to prior and hallowed texts.'

33 Interview with Waldemar Januszczak, *The Studio* 999 (April-May 1983), p23. For a discussion of some of the technological questions raised by Neville's viewfinder, see Bridget Elliott and Anthony Purdy, 'Peter Greenaway and the Technologies of Representation: The Magician, the Surgeon, Their Art and Its Politics', 'Art & Film', *Art & Design*, profile 49, 1996, Academy Editions, London, pp16-23.

34 As Greenaway points out in an interview – in *Cinématographe* 98 (March 1984), pp32-35 – the 1690s mark the beginning of a shift in the status of English painters: as buyers start to acquire paintings domestically rather than from abroad, so English painters begin to show more self-confidence. Neville's peculiar mixture of arrogance and innocence becomes more readily understandable in such a context. As far as the analogy with cinema goes, there is little evidence to show that, in 1982, Greenaway would have thought very differently from Truffaut about English filmmakers, since his unconcealed preference is for French and Italian cinema. (See the interview with Michel Boujut in *L'Avant-Scène Cinéma* 333 (October 1984), pp6,9.) However, as Greenaway frequently states, he is himself a profoundly English artist and heir to a long tradition of English landscape painting, a heritage he explores most fully in *Drowning by Numbers*. This 'nationalist' strain in an otherwise very cosmopolitan filmmaker finds expression in the comic figure of the 'genius loci' or 'green man' of *The Draughtsman's Contract*. This living statue not only provides an ironic comment on the English aristocracy's fad for bringing back classical statues from their 'grand tour' to adorn their gardens; he also, in the film's very last scene after Neville's murder, climbs out of the moat and spits a mouthful of pineapple – a recently imported fruit – at the camera in a gesture which suggests a rejection, both of the film itself with its elaborate games and of the attempt to subordinate the 'spirit of place' to 'imported' disciplines.

FLESH ON THE BONES
Architecture as Allegory

Very early in *The Belly of an Architect* there is a striking night scene in which the principal characters – Stourley Kracklite and his wife Louisa, Io Speckler, his son Caspasian and daughter Flavia, and their friend Frederico Boccini – after dining *al fresco* at a Roman restaurant saunter over to face the Pantheon and end up first sitting, then standing to applaud the red floodlit building as the camera pans slowly across them, registering a variety of attitudes and expressions. The scene is curiously unsettling and raises a number of questions about the relationship between human beings and architecture and, more particularly, about the nature and limits of community and the status of architecture as metaphor. What does it mean to applaud a building? What kind of performance is being enjoyed? What kind of community is formed at the moment a number of individuals come together to form an audience? What is the nature of their attention and their appreciation? What is the relationship between human bodies and buildings? between architecture and filmmaking? These are some of the questions which will guide our discussion of Greenaway's exploration of artistic practice, an exploration which extends throughout his work but finds exemplary expression in this most complex of 'artist films.'[1]

While it is true that a number of Greenaway characters serve as surrogates for the filmmaker – the draughtsman, the surgeon, the cook and the magician come immediately to mind – Greenaway seems to reserve a special place for the architect, as he acknowledges in an interview: *'Belly of an Architect* is in some ways a key movie, and I'm only beginning to understand why. It is extraordinarily autobiographical, and contains all sorts of elements in my cinema practice. I can see me using the cinema like a process of catharsis, working things out for myself. On the whole that's probably quite good, because it really does show that filmmaking for me is not some distant, intellectual exercise, but really gut-related.'[2] In the film, the architecture of Rome functions as one of the main characters: the lives of buildings and people are intricately paralleled and entangled as the architecture of the Eternal City first engulfs and eventually devours the film's central character, Stourley Kracklite, a middle-aged architect from Chicago.

Kracklite is in Rome to curate an exhibition devoted to his longtime hero, Etienne-Louis Boullée, an obscure eighteenth-century French architect. We soon discover that the American, whose career consists of only six-and-a-half completed buildings, closely identifies with Boullée, who is better known for his visionary drawings than for the few structures he actually realised. The exhibition turns into a nine-month gestational nightmare as the cynical Roman fundraisers, who seem to prefer the Italian Piranesi to the French Boullée, siphon money away for other projects, Kracklite's health deteriorates, and his pregnant wife, who is half his age, leaves him for Caspasian Speckler, the architect son of the exhibition's chief fundraiser. The film relentlessly charts the story of

FROM ABOVE
The Belly of an Architect, *The Pantheon;*
Frederico Boccini; Stourley Kracklite; Io Speckler

Kracklite's humiliation on all fronts: as an architect who cannot match the cultural weight and grandeur of Roman buildings; as a middle-aged man with a big belly who cannot compete with the youth or the waistline of his wife's new lover; and as a human body that is being eaten away from within – unlike the seemingly ageless sculpted stone bodies with their heroic abdomens that he obsessively photographs in the streets of Rome. The film ends as Kracklite, dying of stomach cancer and relieved by the Specklers of his responsibility for the exhibition, commits suicide by falling backwards out of a window of the Victor Emmanuel Building onto the roof of Caspasian's car. At the same moment, inside the building, Louisa cuts the tape to open the exhibition, then collapses on the floor, giving birth to a son some nine months after the film's opening scene, in which we saw the couple making love as their train crossed the border from France into Italy.

This brief plot summary gives some indication of the film's more obvious themes: the parallel (and contrast) between artistic creativity and human reproduction; the ephemeral quality of an individual life in relation to cultural and biological continuities; the intertwining of birth and death, health and disease, in the conflicting claims of life and art. Underpinning all these themes is the film's foundational metaphor of the architect as artist figure – and more particularly as stand-in for the filmmaker – and the exploration it allows of the relationship between architecture and the human body, the latter represented metonymically by the contrasting bellies of Louisa and Stourley: one swollen with life, the other bearing only pain and death.

Such topoï, when stated baldly like this, are, of course, anything but new. Architecture has long held a privileged position as metaphor for art in general, possessing typically the

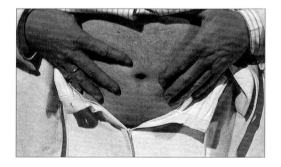

status of inaugural form, as in Hegel's *Aesthetics*: 'Architecture confronts us as the beginning of art, a beginning grounded in the essential nature of art itself.'[3] For Vitruvius, architecture is not only the first of the arts but the one by which all others are judged and the site of convergence of all branches of knowledge. The first chapter of his first book on architecture opens with a portentous statement – 'The architect should be equipped with knowledge of many branches of study and varied kinds of learning, for it is by his judgement that all work done by the other arts is put to the test'[4] – which is parodied in *Belly* by Caspasian as he seduces Louisa: 'Architects ought to know about everything – reproduction . . . gender . . . sex . . . especially sex.'[5] The playful debunking of a sacred text is typical of Greenaway's manner, but it also serves to remind us, however oblique the allusion, of the classical conception of the architect as possessing encyclopedic knowledge; according to Vitruvius, he should 'be educated, skilful with the pencil, instructed in geometry, know much history, have followed the philosophers with attention, understand music, have some knowledge of medicine, know the opinions of the jurists, and be acquainted with astronomy and the theory of the heavens'[6] – qualities which one might well imagine Greenaway demanding of the filmmaker.

Similarly, the relationship between architecture and the human (or, rather, the male) body is a commonplace of the discourse, going back once again to Vitruvius. In his book, *The Architectural Uncanny*, Anthony Vidler traces a 'history of the bodily analogy in architecture, from Vitruvius to the present, [as a] progressive distancing of the body from the building . . . leading insensibly but inexorably to the final "loss" of the body as an authoritative foundation for architecture'.[7] With the lone exception of Le Corbusier's attempt to recreate Vitruvian Man for the twentieth century, Vidler observes, the long tradition of bodily reference seems to have been definitively abandoned with the birth of a 'technologically dependent architecture' and the rise of a 'modernist sensibility dedicated more to the rational sheltering of the body than to its mathematical inscription or pictorial emulation'.[8] Against this trend Vidler notes a recent return to bodily inscription in the work of architects as diverse as Coop Himmelblau, Bernard Tschumi and Daniel Libeskind, all of whom have recourse to the body as metaphor, but to a body quite different from that of Palladian humanism or Corbusian modernism, a fragmented or mutilated body whose 'forms, literal or metaphorical, are no longer confined to the recognisably human but embrace all biological existence from the embryonic to the monstrous; its power lies no longer in the model of unity but in the intimation of the fragmentary, the morselated, the broken'.[9]

Before we try to situate Greenaway's use of the architectural metaphor in relation to this tradition of 'bodywork', a detour through the thought of one of the twentieth-century's most seminal – and, until recently, least acknowledged – cultural theorists might prove instructive. In May 1929, Georges Bataille published the first of a number of short 'Critical Dictionary' articles in the magazine *Documents*. (The 'Dictionnaire critique' project might be described as a para- or anti-dictionary put together in 1929 and 1930 by writers – Bataille and Michel Leiris were the moving spirits – associated with the Acéphale and Surrealist groups; an English translation of the dictionary and related texts has recently appeared under the title *Encyclopaedia Acephalica*.)[10] This 'inaugural' article was a dictionary entry for 'Architecture' in which Bataille denounces the repressive role of architecture in the exercise of authoritarian forms of social control:

The Belly of an Architect

OPPOSITE, FROM L to R
Pantheon; detail of Kracklite's belly; frontal view of Vittoriano

ABOVE
Kracklite's suicide

> Architecture is the expression of the true nature of societies, as physiognomy is the expression of the nature of individuals. However, this comparison is applicable, above all, to the physiognomy of officials (prelates, magistrates, admirals). In fact, only society's ideal nature – that of authoritative command and prohibition – expresses itself in actual architectural constructions. Thus great monuments rise up like dams, opposing a logic of majesty and authority to all unquiet elements; it is in the form of cathedrals and palaces that Church and State speak to and impose silence upon the crowds. Indeed, monuments obviously inspire good social behaviour and often even genuine fear. The fall of the Bastille is symbolic of this state of things. This mass movement is difficult to explain otherwise than by popular hostility towards monuments which are their veritable masters.[11]

Denis Hollier has pointed out the rhetorical slippage in this paragraph which sees architecture progress from being a simple expression of society to playing an active part in the imposition of the order it is supposed merely to reflect. He describes what is created here as a mirror-trap, a structure identifying in advance the object confronting it: 'Architecture, formerly the image of social order, now guarantees and even imposes this order. From being a simple symbol it has now become master. Architecture captures society in the trap of the image it offers, fixing it in the specular image it reflects back.'[12]

The rest of the dictionary article makes plain what is suppressed in this mirror-trap, as Bataille has recourse to the familiar analogy between architecture and the human form; only now, instead of serving to give life to the stone, the metaphor petrifies the human body, reducing it in advance to the articulated whole of the architectural skeleton: 'From human body to monument all that disappears is that which was perishable, which remained in time's power: flesh that rots and its transitory colours. All that then remains is the skeleton, the structure. Architecture retains of man only what death has no hold on.'[13] What architecture denies, what it covers over even as it commemorates death, is the perishability of the human body, its terrible vulnerability, the messy reality of flesh and its inevitable decomposition. Paradoxically, it is the skeleton that hides the corpse. To reverse this movement, to lay bare the humanist lie embodied in architecture, Bataille will transform the ideal proportions of Vitruvian Man, emblem of harmony and unity, into the figure of Acéphale, the headless man, as drawn by André Masson for the cover of the magazine of the same name, the first issue of which was to appear in June 1936. The drawing shows the naked figure of a man, the head severed and displaced – in the guise of a skull – to the sex; a dagger in the left hand, the flaming heart of Dionysos in the right; and in the stomach a coil of gut in the form of a labyrinth.

The resonance of this 'gut-related' discussion with Greenaway's *Belly* becomes even more audible when we recall that two of the other articles written by Bataille for the critical dictionary were 'Musée' and 'Abattoir' – 'Museum' and 'Slaughterhouse'. The first of these starts with an allusion to the origin of the modern museum: 'According to the *Grande Encyclopédie*, the first museum in the modern sense of the word (that is to say the first public collection) would seem to have been founded on 27 July 1793, in France, by the Convention. The origin of the modern museum would thus be linked to the development of the guillotine.'[14] If, in the article 'Architecture', Bataille seeks to explain the frenzy of the mob storming the Bastille in terms of the bloodlust inspired by monuments, he here attempts, again under the sign of the headless man, to explain the appearance of a certain kind of monument – the museum as a space of cultural appropriation and public display – in terms of the purification and expiation of a collective guilt, the ritual cleansing of the body social and politic: 'A museum is comparable to the lung of a great city: every Sunday the throng flows into the museum, like blood, and leaves it fresh and purified.'[15] As with architecture in general, the museum thus functions as a mirror-trap, producing man (*sic*) even as it purports to reflect or represent him through his culture: 'The museum is a colossal mirror in which man contemplates himself, in short, in all his aspects, finds himself literally admirable and abandons himself to the ecstasy expressed in all the art journals.'[16]

As Denis Hollier has argued (in terms which echo Eugenio d'Ors's account of the relationship between classic and baroque), the museum finds its 'other' in the slaughter-

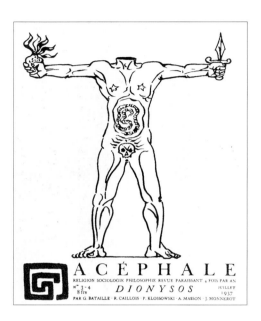

FROM ABOVE
André Masson, Acéphale *(July 1937);* The Belly of an Architect, *Hadrian's Villa*

house, the two together forming a system within Bataille's anthropology of urban space: 'the slaughterhouses are the negative pole, the generator of repulsion, the centrifuge (they are placed farther and farther away from the centre of the city). Museums, the pole of attraction, are centripetal. But within the heart of one the other is hidden.'[17] Or we might have recourse to one of Bataille's favourite organic metaphors, which would encourage us to see here the alternating rhythm of systole and diastole within the pulsating body of the city: the symbiosis of museum and slaughterhouse would then be heard as the rhythm of blood itself as it is pumped round the urban body. 'In our time, nevertheless', writes Bataille, 'the slaughterhouse is cursed and quarantined like a plague-ridden ship,'[18] distanced as a disturbing reminder of the violence on which culture is founded, the repressed memory of all that modernism, with its self-imposed mission of pasteurisation, has tried to expunge in the name of hygiene and purity.

In this respect, it is interesting to recall that Bataille's slaughterhouse is not some metaphorical abstraction, but a working Paris slaughterhouse which is brought before our eyes in all its unaestheticised 'reality' through the photographs of Elie Lotar that accompany the dictionary article. In fact, as Denis Hollier sardonically points out, the slaughterhouse in question is that of La Villette, the very site of Bernard Tschumi's deconstructive 'architecture against architecture' project: in the recycling of the central Paris slaughterhouses of La Villette into a park of science and industry, Hollier's scepticism sees but another phase of the process of modernisation and sanitisation of urban space begun under Haussmann during the Second Empire.

Anthony Vidler is more positive: for him, Tschumi's projects, like Himmelblau's 'architecture of desolation', 'exhibit all the traces of their origins in classical and functional theory, while at the same time constituting an entirely different sensibility'.[19] Yet here again, in Vidler's discourse, we detect the slippage already noted in Bataille's mirror-trap, but this time in reverse: does this architecture produce and impose a new sensibility or does it simply reflect one that already exists? On the one hand, it would seem to 'operate almost viscerally on the body. We are contorted, racked, cut, wounded, dissected, intestinally revealed, impaled, immolated; we are suspended in a state of vertigo, or thrust into a confusion between belief and perception'.[20] But in the very next sentence the slippage is visible: 'It is as if the object actively participated in the subject's self-dismembering, *reflecting* its internal disarray or even precipitating its disaggregation.'[21] And the paragraph's concluding sentence brings us back to the architectural body as image rather than viscerally lived reality: 'The body in disintegration is in a very real sense the image of the notion of humanist progress in disarray.' The hesitations in Vidler's description are revealing and will play a role in our subsequent discussion of Greenaway's own practice, but first let us look in a more general way at what becomes of the bodily analogy in *The Belly of an Architect*.

Perhaps the most positive visual analogy between the architecture of Rome and the human body is the one that plays out on the level not of form but of colour. Sacha Vierny's cinematography combines Greenaway's characteristic frontal approach to the buildings with a sunlit palette that filters out the natural blues and greens of sky and vegetation to render a classical urban landscape in warm flesh tones reminiscent of a healthy human body.[22] Shot in the middle of the day, in bright sunlight rather than shadow,

ABOVE
Abbatoir, *photographs by Elie Lotar from G Bataille, 'Dictionnaire critique',* Documents, *no 6, 1929*

the buildings are so symmetrically framed and isolated by the camera that they come to signify nothing so much as their own aggressively self-confident architecturality. But the profound ambivalence of such a heavily weighted ideological abstraction is hinted at from the start by Wim Mertens's and Glenn Branca's music, which never allows us to think that what we are seeing is a simple celebration of Rome's famous monuments. Greenaway describes Branca's work as a music that bleeds, a wild, raw music that conjures up appalling images of concentration camps, in which one hears fingernails clawing at the walls of the gas chambers.[23] We may be looking at Western civilisation's largest museum, but the music reminds us that the slaughterhouse is not far away (and never has been).

Such suggestions are reinforced by the dialogue which plays repeatedly with the metaphor of a carnivorous architecture: Louisa is the daughter of a Chicago meat-packer; Chicago is the 'city of blood, meat and money', the 'home of the best carnivorous architecture in the Western world' – outside Rome, of course; Kracklite's Chicago-Angelo Building was built entirely on the profit from sausages, is 'a monument to carnivores' and is known locally as the Slaughterhouse. The published script is even more explicit, calling for the undercutting of the camera's 'unashamed celebration' of Rome's architectural heritage with 'several choicely placed references to meat, blood, money and slaughter: the sun's red glow on a statue of disembowellment, on a graphic crucifixion, a glimpse of a butcher's well-stocked shop window, an ornate bank' (*Belly*, p3). However, the most insistent reminder of architecture's ambivalent relationship to death and the mortal body is conveyed through the story of Kracklite himself, whose physical and emotional decline and final disintegration contrast pitifully with the enduring good health of Roman architecture.

Of the two human bodies that are foregrounded in the film, neither is Vitruvian: one because it is a woman's and not a man's;[24] the other because it is overweight, flabby and dying. Moreover, each is metonymically represented by a single part: a belly in which something is growing. But if Louisa, through her pregnancy, finds a way of integrating herself into the space of Roman life with its metaphorics of heritage, continuity and healthy transmission from generation to generation, Kracklite's cancer is living proof of Rome's cynical indifference to individual pretensions, of the carnivorous city's capacity to devour those innocent outsiders who try to take their creativity in unauthorised directions.[25] In the film, the architect's belly is the focus of an essentially visual narrative, the structuring function of which is underscored by the constant recourse to devices of mechanical reproduction in order to chart Kracklite's obsession. Not only does he photograph the abdomens of Augustus and other heroic Roman statues, he litters the floor of his apartment (and of his office in the bowels of the Vittoriano) with dozens of enlarged photocopies on which he draws his own acute discomfort, most often in the spherical shape of the figs that poisoned Augustus, but also on occasion searching for other architectural correlatives amongst the Platonic solids as he describes the sensations in his gut in terms of a sharp-cornered cube or pyramid.

Just as Kracklite's collection of historical and artistic bellies fails to disclose the nature of his illness, his attempt to get the measure of his disease during a hospital visit proves equally unrevealing. Having been told that human intestines are twenty-seven feet long,

The Belly of an Architect

BELOW
Kracklite in a Rodin pose

OPPOSITE, FROM L to R
Augustus's belly photocopy; photocopies on the floor; Kracklite with the doctor; Kracklite in hospital; photocopies on the floor; figs in the belly of Augustus

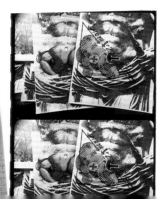

51

he tries to measure out the same length of medical rubber tubing which he winds into coils and presses against his belly. He learns nothing from this exercise and feels sheepish when he realises he is being observed. In the end we recognise the futility of Kracklite's obsessive quest: the comparison of bodies and buildings could go on indefinitely without reaching any conclusions, a point made visually in the screenplay through the juxtaposition of two hospital sequences: the first a televised probe of Kracklite's cavernous intestines, the second showing the patient waking up after the scan and watching a programme about Roman baroque architecture in which cameras slowly pan colonnades whose tunnels of decorative marble recall Kracklite's insides (*Belly*, p78). We are thus brought full circle as the paralleling of buildings and bodies is turned inside out.

The visual recording of Kracklite's intestinal obsession is complemented in the text by the mini-narratives written on the postcards he addresses to Boullée. There we follow an entropic history of decay, the decline and fall of a human body:

#102: My symptoms don't change, only the geography. I used to marvel at the workings of the human body – not any more – consider how clumsy it is – ephemeral, ageing, changing, distorting. The intestines seemed pushed into the stomach cavity anyhow – not neatly coiled and firmly fixed. When the belly's ripped, out they spew like bloated spaghetti pomodoro.

#109: I have become obsessed with the smells of decay: a dustbin of maggots at the Campidoglio, an old woman on the Corso who sleeps on the pavement, the smell of the pissoir by the Spanish Steps, the dried excrement along the Tiber Embankment, the dustbin lorry at the Otello restaurant – yet – with disappointment I have to report that they all smell the same. Decay always, ultimately, smells the same – and I am now identified with it.

#111: I dream of staircases and of tunnels, and believe that my insides must be constructed of faulty architecture and cracked masonry like the Vittoriano or the Palace of Justice, or those suspended arches on the Colosseum – does a baker dream his insides are made of dough and currants, and if he's ill – of stale cake and rotting bread?

Everywhere, in both text and image, the ideal body of architecture is relentlessly undermined: behind the classical facades we smell the corruption of human flesh, behind the museum the stench of the slaughterhouse, as Rome is transformed, through the mediation of Kracklite's dying body, into an allegorical city: 'In the allegory, devoid of symbolic illusion, transience is not transfigured but remorselessly framed into an inescapable *memento mori* of decay. History can only be irreversible decline; and in the allegory its decay becomes permanently accessible to contemplation. This is the essence of the ''ruin'' motif in Baroque literature, where it serves as the perfect encapsulation of natural decline, the fully adequate image of history.'[26]

The analogy between anatomy and geography which is hinted at in postcard #102 is developed as an important motif in the published screenplay but is dropped from the final version of the film. The essence of the analogy is conveyed by postcard #119: 'I've stolen a book of the anatomical engravings of Vesalius. Did you ever hear of him? His bodies are like complicated urban maps of the future.' The corresponding scene in the script proper sees Kracklite flicking through the art books in a large bookstore. He rips

OPPOSITE
Peter Greenaway, postcard collage

BELOW
Prospero's Books, *the belly of Susannah*

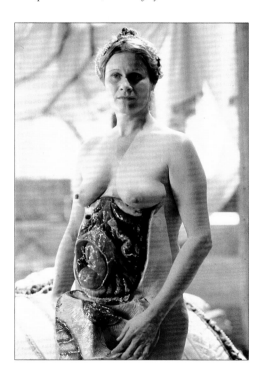

out a coloured reproduction of Bronzino's *Andrea Doria* – the portrait which Flavia pastiches photographically, with Kracklite as Andrea Doria – and secretes it in a hard-cover, oversize edition of Vesalius's *Anatomy* which he then proceeds to steal. Later, as his taxi passes a butcher's shop 'well stocked with red meat', he contemplates the portrait juxtaposed with an 'exploded' view of the stomach (*Belly*, pp87-88). On another occasion, Caspasian and Frederico recount to an uncomfortable Kracklite as they drive through the streets of Rome how a student of American geography had been sitting in the front passenger seat of his girlfriend's car with a large heavy American atlas on his lap; his girlfriend had pulled up sharply at a red light and the book had entered his stomach. 'Pages 67 and 68', explains Frederico, smiling at Kracklite's visible discomfort as Caspasian slams on the brakes and he is thrown forward. 'The Nevada Desert was flooded with his blood' (*Belly*, p58). Kracklite will later find himself once again in the front passenger seat of a car, this time with his stolen hard-cover copy of Vesalius's *Anatomy* on his lap. 'It is opened at a plate showing a half-stripped-down male corpse with the various organs and features of the stomach much in evidence. [. . .] Kracklite experimentally and repeatedly throws his weight against the book corner' (*Belly*, p97).

(The 'other' belly – that of pregnant woman – will appear in one of the 'embodied' tomes of *Prospero's Books*, in a second volume of Vesalius, now lost, that 'is full of descriptive drawings of the workings of the human body which, when the pages open, move and throb and bleed'.[27] It is the illustrations of this *Anatomy of Birth* that draw Prospero into a magic display of organic frame-breaking: 'Beautiful drawings, but – as the pages turn – terrible in their frankness – flayed bodies, severed heads, trepanned skulls, depleted genitalia, dislocated bones . . . the drawings open up to reveal more drawings underneath . . . most of all – of images of procreation. As he turns the pages . . . Prospero's fingers appear to become covered in blood . . . the organs of the body become three-dimensional – small reproductions of the liver, the spleen, the heart, the intestine . . . then red ink floods the page . . . and then black ink.')[28]

If the Vesalius references are missing from the film itself, another (more architectural) intertext is fully developed there. Kracklite's hero is Etienne-Louis Boullée (1728-1799), frequently described as a French 'revolutionary' architect, but known more for his visionary designs and his influence on others than for anything he actually built. His architecture, which he theorised as implementing nature through the use of basic geometric solids, was neo-classical in inspiration, reacting against rococo excess and turning to Roman antiquity for its model of an ideal simplicity and monumentality. Along with his slightly younger contemporary, Claude-Nicolas Ledoux, Boullée was largely responsible for the turn away from the baroque notion of an architecture in which each part of a building must participate in the dynamic flow of the whole; freed from their necessary subordination to the single movement of a whole building, the individual parts, if sufficiently simple and harmonious in their composition, might become autonomous, prefiguring not only the modernist use of architectural modules but also, more circuitously, the postmodern, neo-baroque cannibalising of the architectural corpse. He was particularly fond of the sphere – which he put to stunning effect in his Newton Memorial of 1784, a building that plays such an important part in *Belly* – because it allowed no trick of perspective to alter its formal perfection.

FROM ABOVE
Piranesi, Baths, Hadrian's Villa, Vedute di Roma, *1770;* The Pier with Chains, Carceri, *Plate XVI (second state c1750)*

OPPOSITE, FROM ABOVE
The Belly of an Architect, *Kracklite's exhibition; exhibition preparation in Vittoriano; exhibition preparation in Vittoriano; Foro Italico*

Although he never visited Rome, Boullée was deeply influenced by its architecture, which he knew in part through Piranesi's *Vedute di Roma*. One of the basic structuring devices of Greenaway's film is the use of eight 'architectural' shots, accompanied by appropriately 'architectural' music, to record seven Roman buildings – the Mausoleum of Augustus, the Pantheon, the Colosseum, the Baths of the Villa Adriana, the Piazza and Dome of St Peter's, the Forum, and the Piazza Navona – which particularly influenced Boullée, and one which, by its appearance, suggests that it might well have been influenced by him – the fascist EUR Building constructed by Mussolini in 1942. Greenaway's intention is made clear in the published script: 'The ambition of using these shots – each some 15-25 seconds long (maybe longer) – is to find a powerful visual metaphor for Rome's age and endurance, its architecture seemingly independent of the activities and time-scale of man' (*Belly*, p5). By their sheer grandeur, the buildings are assimilated to a cosmic time – for Boullée, the astronomical time of Newton – which makes the biological time of humans seem ephemeral and derisory by comparison.

It is this impression of a monumental, immutable and inhuman order that leads inevitably to talk of fascism and totalitarianism in relation to Boullée's projects. Kracklite's Italian hosts repeatedly try to needle him with unfavourable comparisons with Piranesi and provocative questions about Boullée's influence on totalitarian architects like Albert Speer. (Piranesi provides a visual subtext in the film as the preparations for the Boullée exhibition transform different parts of the Vittoriano into Piranesi prisons with hanging chains and ropes, ladders, and huge, shroud-like dustsheets. That he is Boullée's 'other' in Kracklite's architectural and personal economy is left in no doubt when the Specklers try to pass off an engraved portrait of Piranesi as a likeness of Boullée, and Kracklite naïvely but predictably rises to the bait.) Ironically, the money that Caspasian is siphoning away from the Boullée exhibition is going to the restoration of the Foro Italico, Mussolini's 'fascist playground', and it becomes clear that the Specklers have no moral grounds for denouncing Boullée as a proto-fascist architect; political principles are mere tokens in Caspasian's world, signifiers emptied of their semantic content so that they might better play their part in the rhetorical manœuvres required for the unrestricted movement of capital. Only Kracklite, it seems, has not broken the habit of thinking politically about history and historically about politics, a facet of his naïveté which comes out in postcard #44: 'Did you ever have to deal with Robespierre? I have a Robespierre and a Danton and an Hébert and a Marat and a St-Just – they are all supposed to be on the same side, but are intent on decapitating one another. Sometimes I am cast as Louis XVI after his capture at Varennes – held in isolation and contempt, brought sandwiches in an underground office that resembles the Bastille.' Once again we note the disquieting proximity, observed by Bataille, of the museum – Boullée designed an enormous one for Paris in 1783 – and the guillotine, of the architectural sublime of Boullée's version of Burke and the political sublime of Robespierre's Terror. Again, too, we think of Benjamin and the allegorical use of the past by artist and revolutionary alike: 'History is the subject of a structure whose site is not homogeneous, empty time, but time filled by the presence of the now [*Jetztzeit*]. Thus, to Robespierre ancient Rome was a past charged with the time of the now which he blasted out of the continuum of history. The French Revolution viewed itself as Rome reincarnate.'[29]

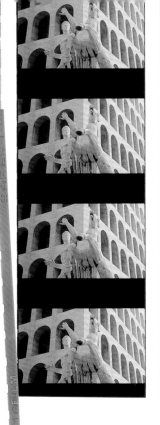

The Belly of an Architect

FROM L to R
*Piazza Navona; Caspasian with Boullée's Tower;
Piazza Navona with Flavia; EUR building;
Kracklite applauding; £ note in cake; Boullée
drawings; Kracklite and two women at
the table; £ note in hand*

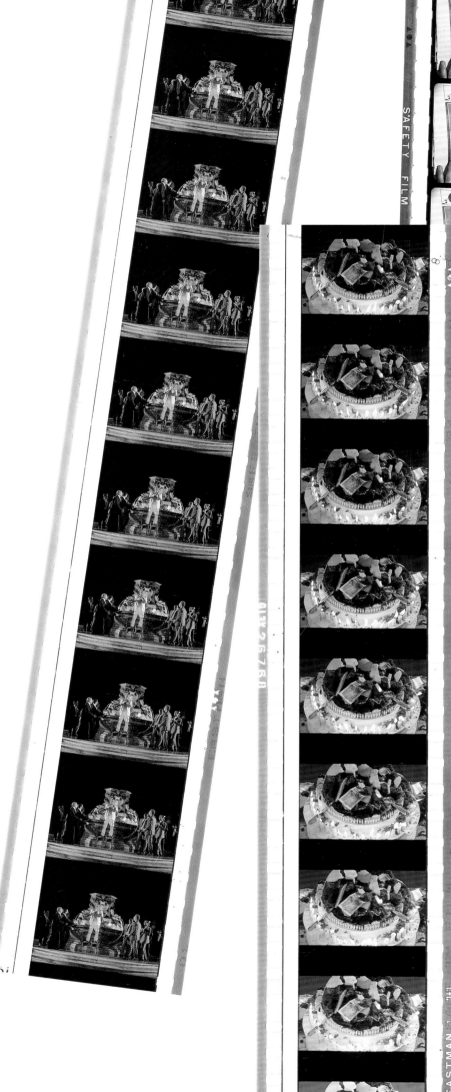

Boullée's architecture may not be any more fascist than it is revolutionary – can any architecture truly be said to be fascist or revolutionary so long as it has not been built, has been put to no use? – but it is certainly *utopian* in the most literal sense of the word: it has, or is, *no place*; that is, it suppresses place – lived, human place – in the name of *space* – Newtonian space which, as we know, is absolute, homogeneous, abstract, universal.[30] Boullée's architecture is a skeleton and, as we have seen with Bataille, it is the skeleton that serves to hide the corpse.[31] What Greenaway's film does, what the architect's belly does (and by that we mean Kracklite's belly, the belly of the actor, Brian Dennehy, who plays Kracklite) is put the flesh – the mortal, vulnerable, perishable flesh – back on the bones and allow it to rot (or, in the case of Louisa's belly, to bear fruit). Kracklite gives Boullée a place, takes him to the Rome he never visited, embroils him in politics (if only those of the art world) and constructs models, simulacra (this is, after all, postmodernity) of his buildings. But he does more than that: he *eats* Boullée's Cenotaph for Newton; he peeps through a keyhole as his rival, Caspasian, cavorting naked with Louisa, sports Boullée's tower as a giant phallus; and he pays his final homage to Boullée's Newton with the manner of his own death, clutching an English one pound note with its portrait of Newton and the apple blossom as he allows gravity to do the rest.

In this respect, the symbolism of the film's first Roman scene – the restaurant terrace with all the main characters at table, immediately before the applauding of the Pantheon – is particularly rich in allegorical detail. With its visual allusions to representations of the Last Supper – *l'Ultima Cena* – it ironically foregrounds a Cenotaph (the cake and icing-sugar model of Boullée's Newton Memorial) which will be eaten by the company like a host. The body being devoured is a triple one – at once Boullée's, Newton's and Kracklite's – as is emphasised by a last lingering shot of the remains of the cake resembling a gutted building; in its ruins burns the English one pound note, Kracklite's good luck token, bearing Newton's portrait.[32] Kracklite's project, the scene tells us, is doomed from the start, as unresurrectible as the (incomplete) project of modernity embodied by both Newton and Boullée; his own ascension will go sadly awry as, here again, flight will prove impossible. One of Kracklite's problems is hinted at, again allegorically, by the burning note: Newton, in addition to his other accomplishments, was for a time Master of the King's Mint, but at the time *Belly* was being filmed the notes bearing his portrait were being pulled out of circulation, signalling the end of an era. Kracklite, unlike Caspasian, does not understand the movement of money in the postmodern, post-Newtonian world and he will pay the price of his ignorance.[33]

Shortly before he dies, Kracklite returns to the restaurant by the Pantheon. Drunk and dispossessed of both wife and exhibition, he staggers about amongst the tables, talking to anyone who will listen (and to anyone who will not) and comes to rest in front of the camera at a table occupied by two horrified middleclass women to whom he shows his belly and explains what is happening inside him. As Greenaway has acknowledged, Brian Dennehy's superlative performance in this scene as a Kracklite coming apart at the seams did much to make him revise his views on the potential role of actors in cinema. In *The Draughtsman's Contract* and *A Zed & Two Noughts*, on his own admission, 'all the actors were essentially signposts to ideas'[34] and he still tends to see himself as 'a painter who's working in cinema', who would rather spend more time with

The Belly of an Architect
Boullée cake

his cinematographer and art department than with his actors.[35] In this sense, a further parallel between architect and filmmaker – and more specifically between Boullée and Greenaway – comes to mind. One of the things that attracted Greenaway to Boullée in the first place was the phenomenon of incompletion, since a filmmaker of Greenaway's kind has fifteen to twenty scripts on the go at any one time, only a few of which will ever see the light of day as finished films.[36] We have already suggested that Greenaway's film, with its obsessive focus on the architect's belly, puts the flesh back on the skeleton that is Boullée's architecture. In the same way, it might be argued that Dennehy's performance as Kracklite fleshes out (literally) the structural and allegorical concerns of Greenaway's approach to film, embodying what might otherwise remain abstract, creating a *place* for the ideas. As Edward Casey would say, there is no place without body and no body without place. In Greenaway's cultural geography of Rome it is the architect's belly (and the death it carries within it – the stench of the slaughterhouse) that breathes new life into the ideal body of classical architecture. In this sense, Dennehy's all too present body might be seen as an intertextual return of the repressed, especially in relation to *The Draughtsman's Contract* with its allegory of the absent body and Neville's naïvely arrogant attempts to empty the landscape of human figures.

Such a reading is reinforced as we follow the weaving Dennehy away from the restaurant and back to the very place in front of the Pantheon where the company of actors had applauded the floodlit building on Kracklite's first night in Rome. Again Kracklite claps and applauds the theatrically lit Pantheon, but this time in a state of solitary exhaustion and acute distress, as though to acknowledge defeat as a crowd of wary waiters and diners try to calm and subdue him. Our suspicions about the 'community' of the earlier scene have been entirely confirmed: we have seen the group fragment into the collection of individuals – each with their own professional and private agendas – which it always was. The scapegoating of Kracklite – from the start the designated sacrificial victim – will allow the others to go on producing their simulacrum of cohesion and stability; and the architecture of Rome, their cash-cow in the postmodern world of commodified spectacle, will continue to receive their tribute.[37]

Once again we are reminded of Boullée, who believed that the circus, rather than the theatre, was the centre of Roman social life and provided the indispensable cement of community. (Thus, when Kracklite asks potentially embarrassing questions about Caspasian's restoration of Mussolini's Foro Italico, Frederico sarcastically retorts that Boullée would have been the first to applaud such a visionary piece of architectural theatre.[38]) It was to the Colosseum that the 'revolutionary' architect turned for inspiration in his drawings for a gigantic amphitheatre which would bring together 300,000 spectators in such a way that they would be the spectacle as well as the spectators. The image is a stunning one and highly suggestive, opening up a number of avenues of reflection. One of these will lead us now to a closer consideration of the role of theatre and spectacle in the films of Peter Greenaway.

NOTES

1 In the introduction to her recent book on film and painting, Angela Dalle Vacche disarmingly writes that most readers will ask why she has not included a chapter on Peter Greenaway: 'My answer is that precisely because a single Greenaway film, *The Belly of an Architect* (1987), explores all the issues I raise in my book, I have chosen to deal with other directors in order to spread my inquiry across many different personalities, instead of collapsing everything into one case study' (*Cinema and Painting: How Art is Used in Film*, University of Texas Press, Austin, 1996, pp7-8). She goes on to say that a discussion of Greenaway would have served as a summary of seven of her eight chapters.

2 Gavin Smith, 'Food for Thought: Peter Greenaway Interviewed', *Film Comment* 26/3 1990, p58. Amongst the 'gut-related' autobiographical details would be Greenaway's own intestinal woes during a short visit to Rome to promote *The Draughtsman's Contract* and the fact that both his parents died of stomach cancer.

3 GWF Hegel, 'Architecture' in *Aesthetics, Lectures on Fine Art*, (trans) TM Knox, Clarendon Press, Oxford, 1975, II, p624. Denis Hollier maintains that, for Hegel, '[a]rchitecture is something appearing in the place of death, to point out its presence and to cover it up: the victory of death and the victory over death. This allows it to be simultaneously the first of the arts – in its empirical, limited form as a stone edifice – and their tomb – in this major and sublimated form: the Hegelian edifice' (Denis Hollier, *Against Architecture: The Writings of Georges Bataille*, [trans] Betsy Wing, MIT Press, Cambridge, MA, 1992, p6).

4 Vitruvius, *The Ten Books on Architecture*, (trans) Morris Hicky Morgan, Dover, New York, 1960, p5.

5 Peter Greenaway, *The Belly of an Architect*, Faber and Faber, London, 1988, p47. All further references to this text will be given parenthetically using the abbreviation *Belly*.

6 Vitruvius, pp5-6.

7 Anthony Vidler, *The Architectural Uncanny: Essays in the Modern Unhomely*, MIT Press, Cambridge, MA, 1992, p70.

8 *Ibid* p69.

9 *Ibid* p70.

10 *Encyclopaedia Acephalica*, comprising the 'Critical Dictionary' and related texts edited by Georges Bataille and the *Encyclopaedia Da Costa* edited by Robert Lebel and Isabelle Waldberg, assembled and introduced by Alastair Brotchie, [trans] Iain White *et al*, Atlas Press, London, 1995.

11 *Ibid* p35.

12 Hollier, p47.

13 *Ibid* p55.

14 *Encyclopaedia Acephalica*, p64.

15 *Ibid*.

16 *Ibid*.

17 Hollier, pxiii.

18 *Encyclopaedia Acephalica*, p73.

19 Vidler, p70.

20 *Ibid* pp78-79.

21 *Ibid* p79. Our emphasis.

22 Amongst the 124 postcards supposedly sent by Kracklite to Boullée and reproduced as an appendix to the published screenplay, two (29 and 36) refer to the colours of Rome as used in the exhibition. Postcard #36 is particularly interesting for its juxtaposition of Rome's 'organic' architecture – 'the colours of human flesh and hair – for the most part warm – orange, orange-red, browns; and warm whites – cream – then warm blacks' – and Boullée's curiously sterile, disembodied black and white: 'I have grown so used to your drawings being in black and white – it's difficult for me to see them in any colour' (*Belly*, p135).

23 Michel Ciment, 'Entretien avec Peter Greenaway sur *le Ventre de l'architecte*', *Positif* 320, October 1987, p24.

24 Although it might be argued that, through the character of Louisa, woman is reduced to an (albeit fruitful) reproductive role as mother while the part of suffering (and sterile) artist falls to her husband, it should be borne in mind that the most productive and successful artist figure in the film is undoubtedly Flavia Speckler, the photographer whose images record both Louisa's progress and Stourley's decline. It is interesting that, when asked about the function of Flavia in the film, Greenaway unequivocally replies that she is there to represent him: a little distant, manipulating events and representing others, more cerebral than emotional. See the interview with Ciment, p23.

25 Louisa's integration into Roman life is constantly stressed in the published screenplay in ways which are only hinted at in the film as it was shot. See, for example, postcard #31.

26 Julian Roberts, *Walter Benjamin*, Macmillan, London, 1982, p143.

27 Peter Greenaway, *Prospero's Books*, Chatto & Windus, London, 1991, p20.

28 *Ibid* p70.

29 Walter Benjamin, 'Theses on the Philosophy of History' in *Illuminations*, (ed) Hannah Arendt, (trans) Harry Zohn, Schocken Books, New York, 1968, p261.

30 For a sustained meditation on the role of place (in contradistinction to space) in our lives, see Edward S Casey, *Getting Back into Place: Toward a Renewed Understanding of the Place-World*, Indiana University Press, Bloomington, 1993. On the virtual or utopian nature of Boullée's architecture, its *placelessness*, Greenaway makes the crucial point in an interview with Don Ranvaud: 'Boullée did extraordinary drawings, but if the buildings don't exist, have not suffered from the effects of weather or changes in fashion, are not subject to criticism for being well or badly constructed, then a final judgment cannot be made' (*Sight and Sound*, Summer 1987, p195). In this respect, Rome, with its infinite recycling of materials and uses, has nothing of the purity of Boullée's functional architecture; the Augusteum, for example, 'has been a fortress, a vineyard, a garden, a bull-ring, a concert-hall, a display ground for fireworks, a dance hall and an air-raid shelter, an arsenal, a prison, a brothel, a barn, a chapel, a stable, a cinema . . . and, of course, a car-park and a public urinal and Mussolini planned to be buried there . . . ' (*Belly*, pp41-42). One is reminded of the extraordinary amount of recycling that goes on in Greenaway's own work, where elements from one project constantly turn up in later ones, refunctionalised but plainly recognisable. Such recycling would seem to be an integral part of a baroque aesthetic of re-membering the corpse.

31 Anthony Vidler takes up the theme of the 'skeleton of architecture' in a remarkable essay on Boullée's 'buried architecture' (*architecture ensevelie*) in *The Architectural Uncanny*, pp167-75.

32 It is interesting that Kracklite did not take the English £5 note as his good luck token, since it bore a portrait of Sir Christopher Wren, the 'English architect's architect' (Peter Greenaway, *The Stairs/Geneva: The Location*, Merrell Holberton, London, 1994, p48).

33 On the interplay of money, space and time in the formation of the modern worldview, see chapter 6 of David Harvey, *The Urban Experience*, Johns Hopkins University Press, Baltimore, 1989, pp165-99. On the passage from modernity to postmodernity, see David Harvey, *The Condition of Postmodernity*, Basil Blackwell, Oxford, 1989.

34 Interview with Don Ranvaud, p196.

35 Interview with Gavin Smith, pp57, 60.

36 In 'Introduction: On Architecture, Production and Reproduction', Beatriz Colomina argues that Ariadne, rather than Daedalus, was the first architect, since while she 'did not build the labyrinth, she was the one who interpreted it; and this is architecture in the modern sense of the term. She achieved this feat through representation, that is to say, with the help of a conceptual device, the ball of thread. We can look at this gift as the "first" transmission of architecture by means other than itself, as architecture's first re-production' (in Beatriz Colomina [ed], *Architectureproduction*, Princeton Architectural Press, New York, 1988, p7). By this token, both Boullée and Kracklite are

architects 'in the modern sense of the term' and the parallel between their architecture and Greenaway's filmmaking becomes even more apparent, especially when we remember that Greenaway, by his own frequent admission, prefers the writing and post-production phases of filmmaking to the actual shooting. In this sense, much of his creative activity might be described as 'virtual'.

37 Coco Fusco, a New York-based curator, sees in Greenaway's film 'an allegory about the inevitable incorporation of cultural products into the manipulations of mass culture. This process is intensified as art institutions and art markets force cultural 'products' into ever more rapid revivalist cycles. Compelled by a constant need to stimulate artistic value, exhibitions like the Boullée show fulfill a specific cultural function, supporting and sustaining their promoters and their institutions far more than they reflect their artistic creators or serve their audience' ('Requiem for an Architect', *Art in America*, February 1988, p35). We shall return to these points in our discussion of Greenaway's own curatorial work.

38 *Belly*, p93. In *The Draughtsman's Contract*, Neville twice applauds the English landscape, thereby turning it, too, into a performance of sorts. When Greenaway, with the help of Reinier van Brummelen, took over Rome's Piazza del Popolo in June 1996 with a spectacular light show to represent the history of the Piazza from Nero to Fellini, the crowds were, according to Julia Owen, delighted: 'The performance [. . .] is greeted each time with storms of applause from the spectators packed into the piazza, some of whom wander in by accident but nearly all of whom stay to watch the show over and over again' (Julia Owen, 'Romans in the Gloaming', *The Times*, 26 June 1996, Arts Section, p40).

SULTAN OR SADIST
The Theatre of Power

The most (in)famous cadaver in Peter Greenaway's work is neither that of the self-defenestrated Kracklite nor that of the scapegoated Neville. It is neither missing in the moat nor suspended on the ceiling, neither drowned nor rotting. It is, however, as baroquely allegorical as they come: the body of a bookseller who has literature rammed down his throat (with a wooden spoon), the corpse of a collector who is stuffed (while still alive) with the pages of his favourite history of the French Revolution, the recycled remains of a reader who is killed for revenge then cooked to take revenge on his killer who had sworn to eat him and is made to do so. The body of Michael – the modest man, the solitary diner, the Thief's Wife's Lover – becomes the unlikely site of an extended bad joke which leaves an equally bad taste in his murderer's mouth; his corpse is transformed into a kind of rebus in a demented child's language game in which letters change places (sometimes in neon: from SPICA to ASPIC, let us say), significations slip and slide in the Thief's torrent of toilet tattle and prurient punning, and metaphors are remotivated, literalised, acted out (in a monstrous charade of ramming and stuffing, cooking and eating) – unpacked as metonymies, as we said before, but here at a pitch of insane cruelty and brutish violence hitherto unsuspected in Greenaway's work.[1] Of all his films, it is *The Cook, the Thief, His Wife and Her Lover* that comes closest to embodying the kind of allegory that Benjamin saw at work in German baroque tragic drama, where, in Julian Roberts's words, '[a]ll the researches and compositions of the human mind never go beyond the perverse riddles of anagrams, onomatopoeic conceits and the rebus; signification ceases to be a power of logos, and becomes itself immired in the brutishness of things – denotation *non verbis sed rebus*.'[2]

It is for the sake of the corpse that Michael dies the way he does, so that he may enter the homeland of allegory; or, as Lévi-Strauss might say, his body is cooked not so that it will be good to eat, but so that it will be good to think with. Resisting the unifying symbolism of the Eucharist, of Holy Communion,[3] the Wife and the Cook prepare a feast, a Last Supper, which takes its meaning from an allegory of enforced cannibalism. In the act of eating Michael, Albert does not receive the Word of God; rather, he is made to eat his own words, which have become flesh so that Albert might see, for the first time, just what he is. Albert, the man of metaphors,[4] is made to take himself literally. Having rammed literature down the booklover's throat, having stuffed the historian with the pages of history, the Thief is made to eat the allegory of the Lover's corpse, to partake of the culture he has raped and murdered. Albert will not live long enough to be redeemed by this human sacrifice, but curiously enough, in this the darkest of Greenaway's comedies, redemption figures more prominently than in any of the earlier films. For if this Last Supper has only one host and one guest, it has a number of wit-

ABOVE
The Cook, the Thief, His Wife and Her Lover,
the death of Michael

ABOVE
The Cook, the Thief, His Wife and Her Lover,
the death of Michael; Michael's cooked corpse

nesses. And at the end of the film these witnesses form a community of kinds, a make-shift rainbow coalition of Albert's victims (including his henchmen) who, inspired by Georgina's example, find communion in death – first Michael's, then Albert's. (This in marked contrast to *The Draughtsman's Contract* and *The Belly of an Architect*, in which it is the artist figure who is scapegoated by a community with which the viewer can have little sympathy.)

For the first time, too, in a Greenaway feature there is no unborn or newborn child to offer the biological hope of redemption through the eternal cycle of death and birth. Neville, Kracklite, the Deuce brothers in *A Zed & Two Noughts*, and even the hapless Bellamy in *Drowning by Numbers*, leave behind the seeds of new life. For Georgina, rendered sterile by Albert's abuse, there can be no hope of redemption through transmission; (symbolic) hope, in true baroque fashion, gives way to (allegorical) mortification and a politically urgent call for redemption now. In this sense, the allegory of *The Cook* is also an exorcism – but an allegory of what exactly? and just what is being exorcised?

To say, as Greenaway himself does and as most critics have been content to repeat, that the film is an allegory of life in Thatcher's Britain, is to claim at once too much and too little. As a political analysis of Thatcherism, *The Cook* would have to be judged unsophisticated and found wanting.[5] But as a theatrical allegory of what it is like to live under a reign of totalitarian Terror, in which power is wielded with capricious unpredictability by a sadistic bully who is at once racist, misogynist, homophobic, anti-Semitic, anti-intellectual, orally and anally fixated, sexually impotent and possessed of the maudlin sentimentality of a Hitler, the story of Georgina and Michael is experienced by the audience as an extraordinarily powerful and passionate performance. From the ritual humiliation of Roy – stripped naked, smeared with dog shit and pissed on by the Thief and his men – to the sudden violence of the fork in the woman's cheek; from the kitchen boy's pathetic willingness to sing on command in his haunting, liturgical soprano to the vicious excision of his navel by a crazed Spica bent on revenge;[6] from the boorish and bombastic vulgarity of Albert's constant prattle to the quiet urgency of Georgina and Michael's lovemaking in unlikely and more or less public locations; from the visually stunning still lifes (modelled on Dutch table painting) and colour-coded and coordinated sets and costumes to the atmosphere of terror and casual brutality that reigns throughout: all this is superbly and self-consciously theatrical, a fact which is underlined by the use of the printed menu to divide the 'play' into acts and by the opening and closing of heavy red curtains at the beginning and end to frame the performance.[7] As Jacobean satire or revenge tragedy,[8] the film is cathartic in that it gives vent to the feelings of frustration and moral outrage shared by many in face of the smug, triumphant philistinism, the greed and rapacity of Thatcherism; as political analysis of the ideology of consumer capitalism it may go no further than angry indictment but that is surely better than silence.

As we have already noted, the first time Greenaway used actors who actually talked to one another on screen was in *The Draughtsman's Contract*. What is particularly interesting about this first venture into dialogue is the fact that Greenaway made a point of using actors with extensive theatre backgrounds rather than actors whose experience was primarily in film. The recourse to Restoration drama as a loose model for the film, the foregrounding of a rich and complex language replete with barbed exchanges and convoluted conceits, and the unusual practice of takes lasting as many as eight minutes instead of a few seconds – all these factors played a part in the decision to use actors trained in the theatre.[9] In the three films which followed *The Draughtsman's Contract*, the theatrical dimension remained present but was significantly upstaged by other structuring devices. It is only with *The Cook* – and subsequently with *Prospero's Books* and *The Baby of Mâcon* – that Greenaway brings us back to the world of explicitly theatrical illusion as a metaphor or allegory of the human condition.

One possible influence that is sometimes cited in relation to *The Cook* and *The Baby of Mâcon* is that of Artaud and his conception of a theatre of cruelty (as expounded most extensively in the essays collected in 1938 under the title *Le Théâtre et son double*).[10] At first sight, the comparison has some merit. Like Artaud's theatre, Greenaway's later cinema might be seen as a kind of total spectacle which has a direct sensory impact on the entire being of the spectator; it rejects psychological realism as a principle of structural coherence;[11] it avoids modern costume; it tends towards a choreographed or, as Artaud would say, a hieroglyphic use of the human body; one of its primary functions is to shock and provoke;[12] it relies heavily on violence, terror and all manner of excess to achieve its ends. But as soon as we look more closely at Artaud's ideas, we are forced to recognise some very fundamental divergences. Artaud's theatre is one of ritual and aura; a sacred, cosmic theatre of communion which cares little for the social and the political, it conceives itself as a plague whose object is to purge collectively the disease that is society. It is a theatre which denies the value of text and language, preferring incantation, noise and gesture (a 'language' of the theatre) to scripted dialogue. It would do away with the author and also with the stage set. More radically still, it would do away with art and literature, denounced as the ultimate expressions of bourgeois conformism. Its aim is to short-circuit reason and induce a kind of hypnotic trance. Clearly, Greenaway's cinema is at odds with many of these tendencies and, despite a certain number of affinities with the twentieth-century tradition of avant-garde anti-theatre – which, in addition to Artaud, would include such names as Jarry, Ionesco, Brook and Grotowski – one would have to look elsewhere for a more adequate theatrical model.

What is missing from the Artaud tradition of a theatre of cruelty is the insistence on critical distance we find, for example, in Brecht's notion of an *epic* theatre, which he was at pains to distinguish from the passive consumerism of what he variously referred to as dramatic, bourgeois or culinary theatre. (The adjective 'culinary' has a very particular flavour as a term of abuse in Brecht's lexicon: the cook as artist is an exemplar of the commodification of art in a consumer society, a point which is not lost on Greenaway's own Cook.) A particularly pertinent discussion of this distinction can be found in Brecht's notes to the opera *Aufstieg und Fall der Stadt Mahagonny*, where the dramatist asks what is needed to create critical distance within that most nostalgic – and culinary – of *Gesamtkunstwerk* forms, the opera. After sketching the different changes of emphasis from dramatic to epic theatre, he raises the crucial question for opera:

> When the epic theatre's methods begin to penetrate the opera the first result is a
> radical *separation of the elements*. The great struggle for supremacy between words,
> music and production – which always brings up the question 'which is the pretext
> for what?': is the music the pretext for the events on the stage, or are these the

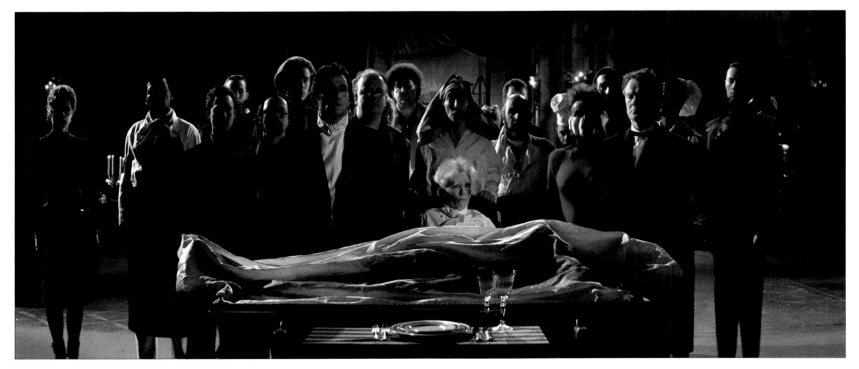

ABOVE
The Cook, the Thief, His Wife and Her Lover,
Albert is made to eat Michael's corpse

ABOVE
The Cook, the Thief, His Wife and Her Lover,
the fork in the cheek; in the parking lot

pretext for the music? etc – can simply be by-passed by radically separating the elements. So long as the expression *Gesamtkunstwerk* (or 'integrated work of art') means that the integration is a muddle, so long as the arts are supposed to be 'fused' together, the various elements will all be equally degraded, and each will act as a mere 'feed' to the rest. The process of fusion extends to the spectator, who gets thrown into the melting pot too and becomes a passive (suffering) part of the total work of art. Witchcraft of this sort must of course be fought against. Whatever is intended to produce hypnosis, is likely to induce sordid intoxication, or creates fog, has got to be given up.

Words, music and setting must become more independent of one another.[13]

This is a lesson that Greenaway has learned well, not only in his own operatic projects,[14] but also, as we argued in Chapter 1, in his feature films where words, music and setting have become increasingly autonomous elements within the total work of art. As a rider to this general observation, we would suggest that the overt theatricality we see in some of Greenaway's films functions to disrupt what Brecht would have called the Aristotelian (that is, empathetic and mimetic) conventions of cinema, in much the same way as Brecht used certain filmic devices to disrupt those same conventions in the theatre.[15] Thus, while *The Cook* mounts a sustained assault on the average viewer's sensibility and produces certain effects which might be seen as cathartic, these elements are ultimately held in check, as in all Greenaway's films, by the demand that the audience remain detached and reflective rather than identifying with what is represented on the screen.

While we are far from thinking that Greenaway's cinema as a whole can be assimi-

BELOW
Rosa

lated to a straightforwardly Brechtian model, it does seem to us that *The Baby of Mâcon* in particular bears strong traces of Brecht's influence. The film's title is that of a morality play that we see being performed in 1659 in a town in northern Italy. The events portrayed in the play are supposed to have taken place two centuries earlier in a French countryside devastated by famine. As we learn from the grotesque, naked figure of the prologue – straight out of Bosch or Brueghel, leprous and lascivious, wearing only a white broad-brimmed cardinal's hat and suspended theatrically in the air on a trapeze-like device – the community has been stricken for years with an infertility that affects not only the crops but also the inhabitants: nothing bears fruit and no babies are born. The play itself will show what happens when a baby *is* born (onstage) to a monstrously obese woman well past childbearing age. The boy child, the 'miracle' baby, will become the site of a struggle for power and wealth, as first his father (who will bottle his fertility and hawk it to actors and audience alike), and then his sister (who will claim to be the child's virgin mother and trade his blessing for produce, livestock and human lives) seek to profit from the infant. Ultimately it is the Church that will gain control and participate as avariciously as anyone else in the child's commodification, auctioning his body fluids to pay for the refurbishment of the cathedral. Resentful at losing her source of wealth and consideration, the sister will suffocate him and be condemned to death by the Church.

The play's audience, which the camera dwells upon at length, is a mixed one of nobles, clergy, local dignitaries, merchants, tradesfolk, peasants and servants, dressed more or less in the costumes of seventeenth-century Italy.[16] The most important spectator is the young Prince Cosimo de' Medici, the future Cosimo III but for the moment a naïve and despotically innocent seventeen year old not quite sure of what to do with the power that is his to exercise.[17] In his essay, 'What is Epic Theatre?', Walter Benjamin reminds us that French classical theatre made room on the stage, amongst the actors, for persons of rank – something the conventions and illusions of modern 'dramatic' theatre would find totally inappropriate. Brecht's epic theatre, however, could not only accommodate the presence onstage of a 'dispassionate observer or "thinker"', it could even give such a figure a central role in the performance.[18] Cosimo, it must be said, is perhaps not altogether the 'dispassionate observer or "thinker"' Brecht had in mind, but he and his entourage certainly play what turns out to be not only a highly visible and audible but also a decisive part in what happens 'onstage' in *The Baby of Mâcon*. With the grave curiosity of a child, he interacts with the actors and interrogates the events as though unable to tell what is real; his comments and questions punctuate the dramatic action with a naïvety of response that prevents us from settling down into the customary comfort of an audience. For while the majority of spectators take their cue from the mid-

The Baby of Mâcon

BELOW, FROM L to R
*mother and child; the birth; the birth; Famine;
staged curtains*

wives who act as a kind of chorus of cheerleaders at a sporting event,[19] leading the audience in counting the contractions as the miracle baby is born to a grotesque old hag or engaging them with the earthy, comic banter of the music hall, Cosimo is there to remind us that these conventions of representation with which everyone seems so comfortable might in fact conceal more about the present than they reveal about the past.

Indeed, everything in *The Baby of Mâcon* functions to underscore the illusory nature of theatrical representation. From the strains of Mouret's Masterpiece Theatre theme music, which accompany the opening credits as we enter the theatre, to the peripatetic prompter in his portable box who polices the performance and voices the lines (and the singing) of the child, everything seems very deliberately designed to tell us not to take anything seriously, to remind us that this is a play and nothing more. It is only after the child's death and the sister's condemnation that things start to go wrong. A law preventing the execution of a virgin is invoked by the midwives to save the girl's life, but Cosimo comes to the bishop's aid with a whispered remedy. His suggestion is well received and leads directly to the girl's rape by 208 $[13 + (13 + 13) + (13 \times 13)]$[20] soldiers blessed by the bishop for doing God's work. The full horror of the situation gradually dawns on Cosimo as he realises that, in this theatre where everything is play-acting and nothing is real, the girl 'playing' the part of the sister really was a virgin, really has been raped 208 times, and really is dead. He is, however, soon consoled and able to enjoy the pleasures of a contrite heart and the absolution of his confessor. The (really) dead child is canonised but then torn to pieces by a mob unwilling to allow the Church the sole benefit of the sacred corpse. The allegorical figure of Famine returns at the end to lament, once again, a time of infertility and great sadness which has befallen the community as punishment for the wrongdoing we have witnessed. However, this is not quite the end, since it is followed by a piece of theatrical bravura as the camera pans out and back from a single child to embrace first the whole troupe of actors, then the audience (including Cosimo and his entourage) which turns and salutes the camera, and then another, larger audience watching the first, which in turn applauds and then turns to greet us, the audience for the film.

The Baby of Mâcon is, then, an elaborate theatrical conceit that recycles a number of the characteristic features of Greenaway's baroque: the allegorical corpse, grotesque as ever, is by now a signature device; the theatrical framebreaking (which started in earnest with *Prospero's Books* as a structural vehicle for exploring the uses and abuses of representation as well as the dangers attendant on confusing reality and illusion) is carried to new lengths and put to more pointed use in this film's conjugation of Brecht with Borges (or Cortázar); the familiar anxiety surrounding the control and marketing of symbolic goods is here extended to the human body itself – and a child's one at that, thereby conflating even more closely than before the themes of artistic production and sexual reproduction. Surprisingly perhaps, given the nature of the violence depicted and the negative reviews the film received, *The Baby of Mâcon* does not carry the same weight of horror and disgust as did *The Cook*, thanks largely to the success of the Brechtian distancing devices. As with the earlier films we have discussed, the slaughterhouse is

once again present as the shadowy 'other' of certain foregrounded social and cultural spaces, but our increased distance from the events portrayed here allows us more time, more room to think allegorically, even on a first viewing. In *The Draughtsman's Contract*, we recall, the allegorical space was the country house of the Whig landed gentry, the architectural emblem of the capitalist ruling class of seventeenth-century England; in *The Belly of an Architect* it was the museum (and the city of Rome) as repository of cultural capital and site of the present's complex negotiations with the past; in *The Cook* it was at once the restaurant, as metaphor for postmodern greed and rampant consumerism, and the book depository as a sanctuary of learning and history that proves all too vulnerable

in times of barbarism; here, in *The Baby of Mâcon*, it is both the (epic) theatre, as a place where illusion is simultaneously produced and laid bare, and the Roman Catholic Church as a theatre of power which tries, on the contrary, to preserve its carefully staged illusions for economic and political gain. The indictment of religious intolerance and the use of rape as a political weapon (with the shadowy presence of Bosnia in the background) is as fierce here as the critique of consumer capitalism in *The Cook*.

The Baby of Mâcon brings us a step closer to understanding Greenaway's treatment of the relationship between author, actor and audience. We recall Benjamin's characterisation of the allegorist as a sultan or a sadist who enjoys enormous power by virtue of his humiliation and dismemberment of the corpse of the cultural past. Is this, then, the role Greenaway plays? Is he, as some critics have suggested, a writer/director on a power trip, humiliating actor and audience alike in his supreme indifference to their needs, treating actors like things rather than people and ramming recycled high culture down the audience's collective throat whether it wants it or not? As far as the actors go, a partial answer can be given straightaway, since their published comments tend to be positively glowing in their praise of Greenaway's direction. Real audiences are obviously trickier to gauge; Greenaway is not everyone's cup of tea and some critics have been outspoken in their denunciation of his cinema, which they find cold and arrogant. We will return to the question of audience and reception in Chapter 6, but now let us reconsider briefly those scenes in Greenaway's films in which actors temporarily become audiences.

In addition to spectators becoming actors and actors becoming spectators in *The Baby of Mâcon*, we have seen Neville applauding the English countryside, Kracklite – alone and with others – applauding the Pantheon, and most of the cast of *The Cook* gathering to witness, if not to applaud, Spica's Last Supper. What should by now be clear is that, in these representations of audiences, Greenaway betrays no desire to reduce the freedom of the spectator or, in Brecht's terms, to 'produce hypnosis', 'induce sordid intoxication', or 'create fog'. The intention is not to throw the spectator into the melting pot of a 'muddled' *Gesamtkunstwerk* so that s/he becomes a 'passive (suffering) part of the total work of art'. Greenaway's conception of the integrated work is resolutely anti-Wagnerian and, although he uses elements of ritual in his films, his cinema has nothing of Artaud's search for an auratic, religious theatre of communion. As we have noted, detachment and separation are the order of the day when it comes to orchestrating the different elements of the *Gesamtkunstwerk*, and the audience is no exception to the rule. The audiences Greenaway represents tend to be independent, relaxed, ironically detached, reflective, sceptical, curious and critical. Their applause, while certainly not in all cases genuine, spontaneous or well-informed, is not a surrender of the will but an exercise of the mind and does not at all belong to a single rhetorical register. The case of Cosimo is crucial here, since it serves as the clearest example of a spectator figure used within the film to mediate the real audience's reactions in an ultimately negative but nonetheless complex way. In so far as he does not take responsibility for the consequences of his intervention, he represents the weakest of audiences morally, although politically the one that wields most power. It is also through him that theatre in Greenaway's films comes closest to the Roman circus so admired by Boullée, where the decision to applaud or not is not simply a question of aesthetic taste but may well be a matter of life or death. As Boullée knew, in such a context the distinction between audience and actors becomes blurred, and the act of applauding functions as both a performance and a performative, since it produces an effect in the real world.

The film that deals most explicitly (and in explicitly theatrical terms) with the refusal of what Brecht calls 'witchcraft' is *Prospero's Books*. Since it is one in a very long line of adaptations of Shakespeare's *The Tempest*, any discussion of the film will almost inevitably focus on what is new in Greenaway's version. Two things stand out: the film is the

The Baby of Mâcon
OPPOSITE, FROM ABOVE
audience; Cosimo de' Medici and audience;
Cosimo intervenes; Cosimo intervenes

ABOVE
the prompter

director's most ambitious attempt to create a *Gesamtkunstwerk* in the Brechtian sense, incorporating elements of dance, opera, elaborate set and costume design, and a heavy use of art historical allusion and quotation; it is also the occasion for an exploration of certain new technologies. Our comments will confine themselves to the intersection of these two facts with the problem of power in the relationship between author, actor, filmmaker and audience.[21]

In recent years, Greenaway has enthusiastically embraced the idea of incorporating new technologies into the production of cinema, partly as a result of his experience of working for television, where he first discovered the seductions of the Quantel Paintbox while producing *A TV Dante* for Channel Four. *Prospero's Books* grew out of this experience as an attempt to marry the technologies of the digital paintbox and high-definition television on 35mm. In his enthusiasm for the new combination, Greenaway might almost be mistaken for a McLuhanite techno-optimist:

> The script of *Prospero's Books* calls for the manufacture of magical volumes that embody their contents beyond text and conventional illustration. Prospero, sixteenth-century scholar and magus, would no doubt call upon the most contemporary state-of-the-art techniques that the legacy of the Gutenberg revolution could offer. The newest Gutenberg technology – and to talk of a comparable revolution may not be to exaggerate – is the digital, electronic Graphic Paintbox. This machine, as its name suggests, links the vocabulary of electronic picture-making with the traditions of the artist's pen, palette and brush, and like them permits a personal signature. I believe its possibilities could radically affect cinema, television, photography, painting and printing (and maybe much else), allowing them to reach degrees of sophistication not before considered.[22]

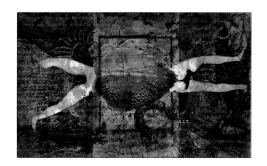

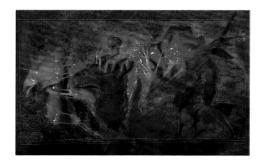

Prospero's Books

ABOVE and OVERLEAF
paintbox images

However, while he claims that no special technical ability is necessary to operate the machine and that competent familiarity can be quickly attained, Greenaway acknowledges that 'its potential, as always, depends on the audacity, imagination and pictorial sophistication of the user'. This is a point he makes even more strongly in an interview with film critic John Wrathall: 'The actual technology *per se* doesn't necessarily make a product that is valuable, of course; it's the imagination and resources that are put into it. And you have to be careful that it doesn't become all technology and nothing else. Technology should just be the tool and not the master.'[23]

What is particularly interesting in this and similar statements by Greenaway is the implicit claim that, in the last analysis, the artist is indeed the master. Such an assumption would seem to fly in the face of Raymond Williams's contention that, for it to be truly democratic, a new technology should enable the ordinary individual to be a producer rather than just a passive receiver of culture.[24] Indeed, the entire structural premise of *Prospero's Books* would seem to contradict such a position, since the film turns around the figure of an all-powerful magician-illusionist – as variously embodied in Prospero, Shakespeare, Gielgud and Greenaway – and his ability to make worlds out of word and image, to create a virtual reality in which others will be caught and, if necessary, disciplined and punished. In this sense, the reading of power in the play which, in most postcolonial productions and interpretations of *The Tempest*, has focused almost exclusively on the Prospero-Caliban relationship, is here displaced onto the question of textual control and technical mastery. This is in large part achieved by two important innovations: the casting of dancer Michael Clark as Caliban allows that character an unusual degree of artistic autonomy and presence in the film, so that we do not see him simply as the colonised 'other'; as though to compensate for this diffusion of interest (symptomatic of the separating out of elements in the Brechtian *Gesamtkunstwerk*), Prospero himself appears as the author of the play, penning the words as they are spoken and, for the first four acts, voicing all the parts himself. This exploration of the relationship between written and spoken word,[25] between author and actor, is constantly foregrounded by the film's play with mirrors and frames, which are repeatedly revealed to be not what they seem,[26] and by the complex cross-identifications between Prospero and his inventors and interpreters – Shakespeare, Gielgud and Greenaway. The struggle for power centres obsessively around questions of authorship, performance and representation.

Moreover, Greenaway's enthusiastic embracing of the Paintbox technology is not without ambiguities of its own, since what the electronic paintbrush paradoxically makes possible is a return to an earlier, more artisanal form of artistic production: 'I started life as a painter and I still believe painting is the supreme experimental visual art form. But there's a way that this [Quantel] not only combines the languages of television and film but also brings back painterly values, which is very exciting. The Paintbox, as its name suggests, links the vocabulary of electronic picture-making with the tradition of the artist's pen, palette and brush. Now I know that cinema is not painting and vice-versa, but there's a whole language there that can be used in cinematic terms and that can make the cinema a thousand times more exciting and interesting.'[27] But what exactly does Greenaway hope to achieve in his use of the digitally artisanal Paintbox? Is he simply seeking a way to resuscitate Old Masters who have little or nothing to say to our own times, to reinscribe the techniques and values of a nostalgic and conservative 'high' art in the infinitely reproducible forms of electronic culture? Or is he attempting a serious exploration of the politics of cultural technologies, a stocktaking and diffusion of cultural archives,[28] and a questioning of the necessity and sufficiency of technical mastery and its relation to political and artistic vision?

We shall come back to these questions in a more general way in Chapter 6. For the moment let us simply note that Prospero is, in this respect, a curiously ambivalent figure, since, for all his colonising ambitions, he comes to recognise his limitations as a magician and a man, a point which is underscored at the end of the film when, abjuring his 'rough magic', he drowns his books and turns, in close-up, to the audience, thereby breaking any last remains of filmic illusion, and appeals to us to release him from the world he has created with our consent and cooperation:

> Gentle breath of yours my sails
>
> Must fill, or else my project fails,
>
> Which was to please.

Prospero's (and Greenaway's) 'insubstantial pageant' is over. It was, after all, only a play, as Greenaway's theatrical films have been reminding us since the living statue spat pineapple at the camera at the end of *The Draughtsman's Contract*. As to whether Greenaway pleases or not, that is for us and us alone to decide. What mastery he has is over materials, not minds, a point he has always been at pains to stress.

BOOK OF

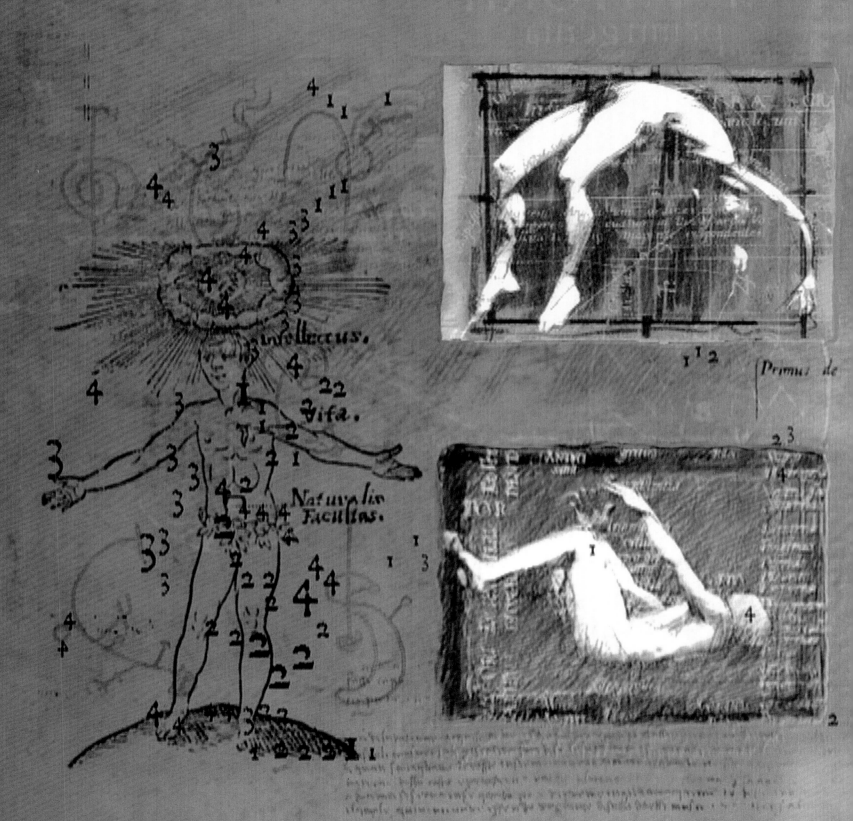

MOTION

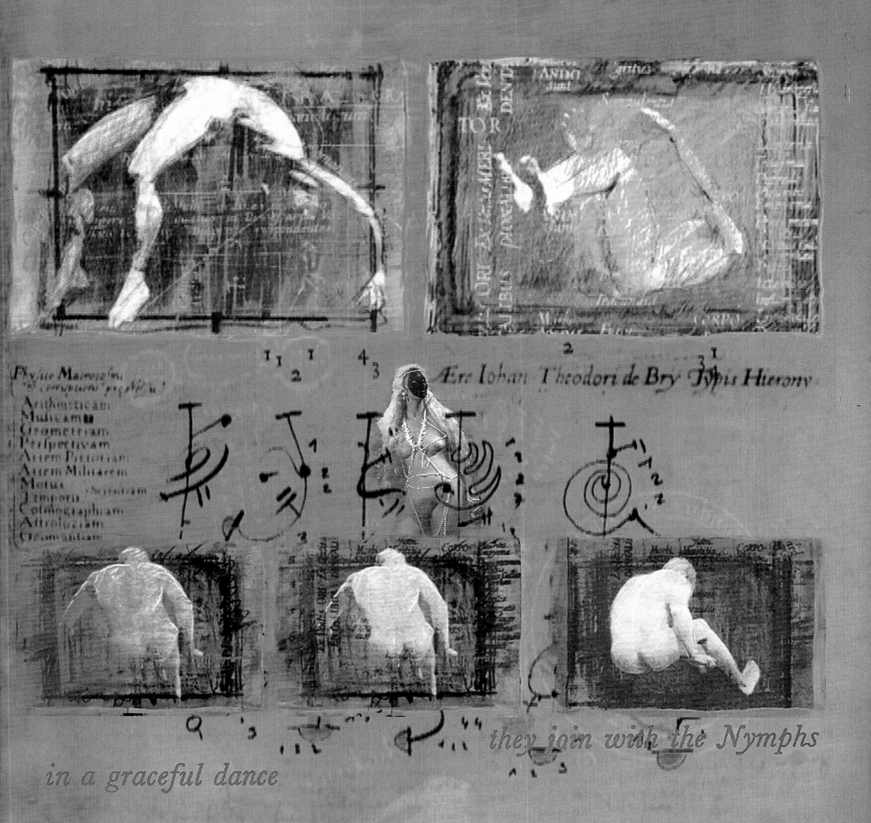

in a graceful dance

they join with the Nymphs

NOTES

1 Michael's death and subsequent fate are textually produced as the culmination of a series of metaphorical one-liners generated from the mixing of two implied (though unstated) metaphorical commonplaces: You are what you read *and* You are what you eat. (There is a small chain of bookstores in Ottawa called 'Prospero – The Book Company' whose slogan is: 'We are what you read'. One imagines Greenaway would smile.) 'This is a restaurant, not a library' is the Thief Spica's refrain. 'Reading gives you indigestion', he admonishes his Wife's Lover. 'Didn't you know that? Don't read at the table!' 'What good are all these books to you?' asks Georgina in turn. 'You can't eat them.' But, of course, Michael does.

2 Julian Roberts, 'Melancholy Meanings: Architecture, Postmodernity and Philosophy' in Nigel Wheale (ed), *The Postmodern Arts*, Routledge, London, 1995, p139. The rebus, of course, has affinities with the hieroglyphic logic of dream and the unconscious. More particularly, the process of semiotic remotivation is characteristic not only of the dreamwork but also of aphasia, schizophrenia and other forms of psychic and linguistic breakdown or regression. Thus, the delirious ideas of schizophrenics can be interpreted as *lived metaphors*. For a good account of linguistic remotivation, see Ivan Fónagy, 'Motivation et remotivation. Comment se dépasser?', *Poétique* 11, 1972, pp414-31.

3 When Georgina first approaches Richard, the Cook, with her unusual request, he mistakenly assumes that she will be the one to eat Michael as a means of achieving eternal communion. She corrects him 'with a broad grin' (*The Cook, the Thief, His Wife and Her Lover*, Dis Voir, Paris, 1989, p88). Later, when confronting Albert with the cooked body of Michael, she tells him: 'No, Albert – it's not God – it's Michael.'

4 It is Albert who has to explain the difference between literal and metaphorical meanings to his acolyte Mitchel during the murder of Michael.

5 Michael Walsh has an interesting analysis of some of the problems posed by the film as an allegory of Thatcherism. See Michael Walsh, 'Allegories of Thatcherism: The Films of Peter Greenaway' in Lester Friedman (ed), *Fires Were Started: British Cinema and Thatcherism*, University of Minnesota Press, Minneapolis, 1993, pp255-77.

6 Another example of a metaphor being acted out according to Spica's insane logic of literal-isation: Pup's belly button is cut out because it might serve to 'button' or 'unbutton' his lip.

7 The opening is particularly interesting, since the ritual pulling back of the curtains (onto the parking lot as cars roar up and Spica and his gang get out to humiliate Roy) follows a long, slow vertical tracking shot (the only one in a film held firmly in the grip of the horizontal) which takes us up through the Brechtian scaffolding below the sound set to ground level.

8 Greenaway's own comparison is with John Ford's *'Tis Pity She's A Whore*, which saw at least two revivals in Britain in the late eighties. Susan Bennett prefers to see *The Cook* as a satiric city comedy rather than a revenge tragedy (Susan Bennett, *Performing Nostalgia: Shifting Shakespeare and the Contemporary Past*, Routledge, London, 1996, p102).

9 On the use of theatre-trained actors in *The Draughtsman's Contract*, see, for example, the interview with Robert Brown in *Monthly Film Bulletin* 586, November 1982, p256.

10 During his lifetime, Artaud's ideas had little impact but since his death in 1948 they have enjoyed several waves of popularity. Perhaps the most important for Greenaway would have been Peter Brook's productions of Shakespeare's *King Lear* and Peter Weiss's *Marat/Sade* in the late sixties.

11 The one instance in *The Cook* where this principle does not hold is Georgina's monologue to the dead Michael, in which she tries to 'explain' her marriage by describing her own past humiliations as the object of Albert's perverse desires. For some viewers, this scene is the film's saving grace as it 'humanizes' certain behaviours; for us, it is an uncharacteristic lapse into the relative banality of psychological explanation that compromises the film's structural integrity.

12 Such provocation is not, of course, peculiar to the theatre of cruelty. The historical avant-garde made telling use of shock tactics and AR Braunmuller's introduction to the English edition of *Aufstieg und Fall der Stadt Mahagonny* starts with the following sentence: '*The Rise and Fall of the*

City of Mahagonny must offend and repel its audience if it is to succeed' (Bertolt Brecht, *The Rise and Fall of the City of Mahagonny*, [trans] WH Auden and Chester Kallman, David R Godine, Publisher, Boston, 1976, p9).

13 *Brecht on Theatre: The Development of an Aesthetic*, edited and translated by John Willett, Hill and Wang, New York, 1964, pp37-38.

14 *The Death of Webern and Others* is a projected ten-part opera about the deaths of ten modern composers, both fictitious and real, to be performed in ten different cities with music by ten different composers. The first one, *Rosa*, was produced in Amsterdam in 1994.

15 On Brecht's use of cinema, see Maria Shevtsova, *Theatre and Cultural Interaction*, Sydney Studies in Society and Culture, Sydney, 1993, Chapter 8, pp137-50.

16 These characters reappear in the guise of a hundred photographic portraits in *The Audience of Mâcon*, an exhibition Greenaway curated in 1993 at the Ffoto Gallery in Cardiff.

17 The name is not chosen at random. Almost the last of the great Florentine family, the young Cosimo is a sentimental religious fanatic, heavily influenced by the Counter-Reformation and his mother's pious intolerance (Peter Greenaway, *The Baby of Mâcon*, French translation by Christophe Marchand-Kiss, Dis Voir, Paris, 1994, p7). He is also, ironically, the son of Cosimo II, a man of reason and scientific curiosity and patron of Galileo, as we recall from Brecht's 1938 play, *Leben des Galilei*, in which he appears as a nine-year-old boy.

18 Walter Benjamin, 'What is Epic Theatre?' in *Illuminations*, (ed) Hannah Arendt, (trans) Harry Zohn, Schocken Books, New York, 1968, p149.

19 The theatre as sporting event is not only a very Brechtian metaphor (and device) but also recalls Boullée's preference for the Roman circus over its theatre.

20 The formula is an allegory of historical and legendary abuse. See *The Baby of Mâcon*, p111.

21 We have discussed the politics of Greenaway's use of new technologies in 'Peter Greenaway and the Technologies of Representation: The Magician, the Surgeon, Their Art and Its Politics', 'Art & Film', *Art & Design*, profile 49, 1996, Academy Editions, London, pp16-23. Our brief comments here reprise some of those main points.

22 Peter Greenaway, *Prospero's Books*, Chatto & Windus, London, 1991, p28. This quotation comes from a detailed description of how the film's paintbox images were made (pp28-33).

23 John Wrathall interview with Peter Greenaway, 'Mosaic mindscapes', *Screen International*, Sept 13-19, 1991, p18.

24 Raymond Williams, 'Culture and Technology' in *The Politics of Modernism: Against the New Conformists*, Verso, London, pp119-39.

25 As Maurice Yacowar has pointed out, the disjunction between written and spoken language is foregrounded in the scene in which we see Prospero writing the play's first word – 'Boatswain?' – only for it to be immediately contested by Gielgud's spoken 'Bosun?' (Maurice Yacowar, 'Negotiating Culture: Greenaway's *Tempest*', *Queen's Quarterly* 99/3, Fall 1992, p694). This is a simple reminder that the written and spoken word are not to be confused, that language, too, here obeys the Brechtian principle, and that we are expected to remain detached observers.

26 As Greenaway writes in his introduction to *Prospero's Books*, 'This framing and re-framing becomes like the text itself – a motif – reminding the viewer that it is all an illusion constantly fitted into a rectangle . . . into a picture frame, a film frame' (p12). Cf Alba's self-composed epitaph in *A Zed & Two Noughts*, after she has had her second leg amputated: 'here lies a body cut down to fit the picture.'

27 Greenaway in Wrathall, p18.

28 Greenaway's strong claims for painting are well known: 'The history of painting is one of borrowing and reprising, homage and quotation. All image-makers who have wished to contribute to it have eagerly examined what painters have done before and – openly acknowledged or not – this huge body of pictorial work has become the legitimate and unavoidable encyclopedia for all to study and use' (*Prospero's Books*, pp12-13).

(UN)NATURAL HISTORIES
Collecting Cultures, Crossing Limits

Peter Greenaway's work is perhaps most usefully seen as a continuing exploration and transgression of the limits of representation. The taxonomies we use to order our store of knowledge; the technologies that shape our cultures; the buildings that display and perform our artefacts; the aesthetic, moral and political codes that prescribe what can and what cannot be represented and in what ways: all are scrutinised, played with, turned inside out and upside down in an attempt to open new spaces and produce new meanings. This chapter will trace some of the transgressive activities that take as their site the interface between filmmaking and curating. It will focus on two sets of concerns, which can be represented, for the moment, by two questions: what do we make of books that rely less on the mediation of language than on their own materiality (and even corporeality) to represent the world and make their point? and what happens when the vocabulary of cinema is exported first to the museum, then to the streets and buildings of a major city? Our discussion will close with a consideration of the act of collecting and its obsessive presence in Greenaway's films and exhibitions alike.

The conjunction of books and bodies has frequently played an important part in the feature films. Michael's gruesome death in the book depository and Kracklite's tentative experiments with a stolen *Vesalius* have been discussed at length, but bookselling had already figured in an earlier film, *A Zed & Two Noughts*, again in an anatomical context, though sexual this time rather than alimentary. When Venus de Milo, a prostitute who would like to earn a living as a pornographic storyteller, is asked by Oliver Deuce if she has ever done it with animals, she replies evasively that, if it would help, if it is what he wants, she could invent: 'It'll cost four pounds a story. That's what Anaïs Nin charged in 1927 – only she did it professionally. I haven't started professionally yet. Four pounds . . . or an introduction to a publisher, or a credit note to any large bookshop or . . .'[1] Later she tells Oliver's twin brother, Oswald, that her rate is five pounds for animal stories or sixty for ten thousand words, 'one eighth of what Pauline Reage got for the *Story of O*. I'm very reasonable. Or you can have it free if you can find me a publisher'. Later still she will claim that Beardsley was paid sixty guineas for what Venus did to the unicorn in *Under the Hill*, and before the end of the film she will see her story 'The Obscene Animals Enclosure' in print, thanks to the intervention of the mysterious Felipe Arc-en-Ciel.

In all these films, the relationship between book and body seems to participate in a general tendency of Greenaway's work to mingle mind and matter, high and low, to dissolve the distinctions between the body and its representations, between nature and culture; if books can be the object of a(n) (un)natural process of ingestion, digestion and defecation, they can also be traded like flesh on the meatmarket of culture, reminding us once more of the symbiotic relationship between museum and slaughterhouse: 'This

OPPOSITE
The Audience of Mâcon

BELOW
A Zed & Two Noughts, *Venus de Milo and Felipe Arc-en-Ciel*

needs cooking', says Spica aggressively, of a book, while Venus de Milo's trade in pornographic invention intersects curiously with that in animal body parts.[2] Crossovers of this kind abound in Greenaway's films: in *The Cook*, while high culture is ritually consumed through the French menus and artfully posed Dutch table paintings of the restaurant, *Le Hollandais*, it is constantly brought low by Spica's bombastic vulgarity. 'This custard's salty', he complains of the hollandaise sauce, while boasting with a leer that he has 'always been able to understand French letters'.

We have seen that the central conceit of *Prospero's Books* calls for 'the manufacture of magical volumes that embody their contents beyond text and conventional illustration'.[3] The books are twenty-four in number, furnished by the good Gonzalo at the time of Prospero's exile. They are not only the source of Prospero's magic but are themselves endowed with a magical life of their own. Thus, the pages of *The Book of the Earth* are 'impregnated with the minerals, acids, alkalis, elements, gums, poisons, balms and aphrodisiacs of the earth. Strike a thick scarlet page with your thumbnail to summon fire. Lick a grey paste from another page to bring poisonous death'.[4] When *The Book of Colours* is opened at a double spread, the colour is translated into a direct sensory experience. 'Thus a bright yellow-orange is an entry into a volcano and a dark blue-green is a reminder of deep sea where eels and fish swim and splash your face.'[5] Such correspondences find their ultimate expression in *The Book of Universal Cosmography* which 'attempts to place all universal phenomena in one system'; here we find 'catalogues arranged on a simplified body of man, who, moving, sets the lists in new orders, moving diagrams of the solar system. The book deals in a mixture of the metaphorical and the

BELOW
Prospero's Books, *Books. From L to R:* Love of Ruins; End-Plants; A Bestiary of Past, Present and Future Animals

scientific and is dominated by a great diagram showing the Union of Man and Woman – Adam and Eve – in a structured universe where all things have their allotted place and an obligation to be fruitful'.[6] Other books are more graphically embodied. *The Autobiographies of Pasiphae and Semiramis* is a pornography whose pages are 'scattered with a sludge-green powder, curled black hairs and stains of blood and other substances'.[7] Since the pages leave acidic stains on the fingers, it is advisable to wear gloves when reading the volume. *A Book of Motion*, on the other hand, is always bursting open of its own volition and has to be buckled tightly shut with leather straps and held down at night with a brass weight.

While some of Prospero's books do contain stories, the logic which animates them is, by and large, not that of narrative but of analogy or metaphor; their mode of representation has less to do with plotting than with direct (imagistic or sensorial) embodiment. In this, they resemble the objects of an exhibition Greenaway curated in 1992 for the

Viennese Akademie der bildenden Künste. The exhibition's ironic premise was that it should be possible to represent the world using only one hundred objects: 'A museum, a gallery, a collection of artefacts assembled in one space, with one idea, one heading, from one curator – is a sort of representation of the world. This one mocks human endeavour by seeking to be totally representative encyclopedically – but in brief. It takes care of scale and time, masculine and feminine, cat and dog. It should leave nothing out – every material, every technique, every type of every type, every science, every art and every discipline, every construct, illusion, trick and device we utilise to reflect our vanity and insecurity, and our disbelief that we are so cosmically irrelevant.'[8] To achieve such a Borgesian ambition, two things are necessary: the logic of the exhibition must be one of analogy and association, and it must make use of internal mirrors.

The associative organising principle could be illustrated by almost any of the hundred descriptions that accompany the objects.[9] Object #9 ('A Fallen Tree') will serve as a particularly pleasing (because formally mimetic) example of this (potentially infinitely) branching logic: 'A fallen tree, complete with roots and branches, laid on its side, to illustrate what was vertical is now horizontal, to demonstrate falling and the fallen, to represent trees, roots, branches, the phrase "root and branch", the metaphor of the branching of species in Darwin's understanding of the evolutionary system, the concept of a family tree, an acknowledgement of gravity, the death of the South American rain-forest.' The encyclopedic ambition of exhaustivity is ironically signalled by Object #79 ('A Collection of the Bones of the Ears of Birds')[10] and the arbitrary nature of taxonomies by Objects #37 ('100 Red Books') and #45 ('The Alphabet'). The colour red is chosen

100 Objects to Represent the World

FROM L to R
A fallen tree; a collection of bones of birds' ears; 100 red books

arbitrarily to preclude the kind of chaotically heterotopian orderings that overworked librarians have nightmares about: ' . . . books can also be catalogued by the total sum of their pages, by the numerical proportion of upper to lower case letters, by the number of times any particular word appears, by the evidence of mould and the prevalence of yellowing paper.'[11] The alphabet is one of Greenaway's favourite structuring devices, used for example in *H is for House* and *A Zed & Two Noughts*, and reproduced here along a long wall in letters at least half a metre high to remind us of the absurdity of our systems of ordering and organisation: 'By the English use of this system of codes, it is curiously possible to place the disparate concepts represented by Hell, Heaven, happiness, health, His Holiness, hysterectomy, Hitchcock, Hitler and hiatus in one bracket and under one section.'

Alongside the constitutive elements of text we find, predictably, the allegorical corpse, here represented in two forms: Object #66, the decomposing corpse of 'a recently

OVERLEAF
The Physical Self, *shoes and feet*

PAGE 86 ABOVE
100 Objects to Represent the World, *a dead cow*

PAGES 86 BELOW and 87
The Physical Self, *naked man in case; United Colours of Benetton; naked woman in case*

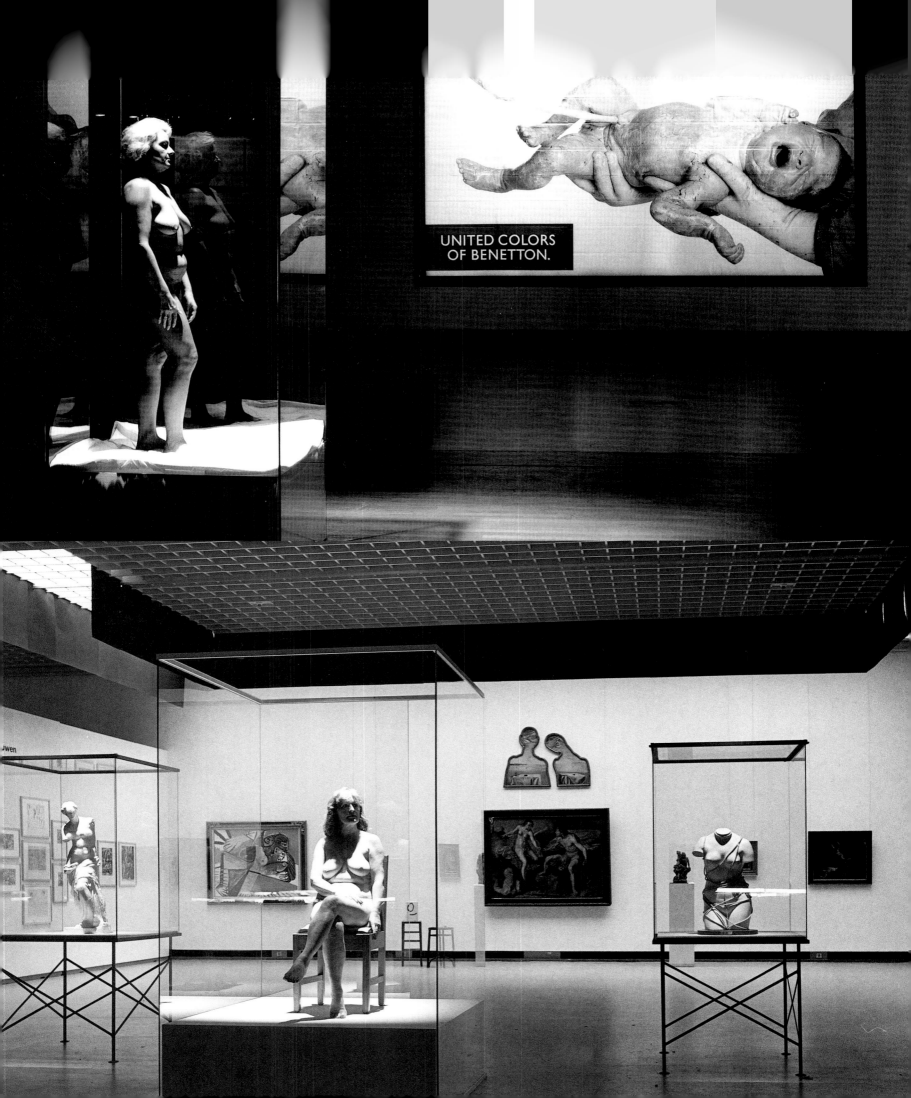

UNITED COLORS
OF BENETTON.

killed cow intended for the slaughterhouse' and Object #73, a dissected and dismembered human body: 'Let us consider a minimum of 20 parts – head, torso, belly, two arms, some separate fingers, genitals, upper legs, lower legs, feet and some toes.'[12] The show also includes a live baby, accompanied by its mother, recalling the four unclothed human bodies in different poses that Greenaway had exhibited in glass cases in *The Physical Self*, held in Rotterdam's Boymans-van Beuningen Museum in 1991. The introduction of live – as well as dead – human and animal bodies, alongside cultural artefacts of various kinds, is just one way in which the relationship between cinema, theatre, museum and slaughterhouse is put forth for contemplation.

The objects representing different kinds of ordering principle can be seen as functioning self-referentially as internal mirrors, as can Object #30 ('The Willendorf Venus'): ten fake versions of the 'fake' Venus displayed to 'demonstrate the museum trade in the reproduction of cultural objects for money'. Such devices remind us of the second of Prospero's books, a *Book of Mirrors* containing some eighty mirrored pages made of many different reflective materials. 'Some mirrors simply reflect the reader, some reflect the reader as he was three minutes previously, some reflect the reader as he will be in a year's time, as he would be if he were a child, a woman, a monster, an idea, a text, or an angel. One mirror constantly lies, one mirror sees the world backwards, another upside down. One mirror holds on to its reflections as frozen moments infinitely recalled. One mirror simply reflects another mirror across a page. There are ten mirrors whose purpose Prospero has yet to define.'[13] The strategic use of internal mirrors, as artists from Velásquez to Dali and writers from Valmiki to Borges have discovered, can

FROM ABOVE, L to R
Prospero's Books, *Prospero seated with frame*;
100 Objects to Represent the World, *exhibition catalogue*; The Pillow Book, *Nagiko and Jerome; Nagiko as a child*

The Pillow Book
OPPOSITE, FROM ABOVE, L to R
Nagiko as a child with painted face; Nagiko being written on; Nagiko with writing; Nagiko writing

produce remarkable representational effects, not least the illusion of infinite reduplication suggested, for example, by Dalí's *Unfinished Stereoscopic Picture* or Borges's 'Partial Magic in the *Quixote*', or, more disturbingly, the kind of paradoxical or aporetic *mise en abyme* exploited by some Escher prints or certain short stories by Cortázar, in which a fragment is made to include the whole of which it is a part, thereby transgressing the boundaries separating different logical levels of representation.[14] Greenaway's Vienna exhibition has its own Borgesian mirror, Object #100 ('The Exhibition Catalogue'), the description of which starts with a loose paraphrase of Mallarmé ('It has been said that all the world exists to be put into a book') and continues with the following instruction: 'Exhibit 100 will be the catalogue of the exhibition, displayed under a spotlight on a two metre high white marble pedestal, under a cubic glass case approached by three small steps on all four sides. It will be open at the page that comments on Exhibit 100 that shows the Exhibition Catalogue open at the page that comments on Exhibit 100 that . . .'[15]

The relationship between text and body (both alive and dead) is explored again in Greenaway's most recent feature film, *The Pillow Book*. The film tells the story of Nagiko Kiohara, a Japanese girl growing up in Kyoto in the 1970s and 80s. Her father is a writer and calligrapher who, every year on her birthday, writes a birthday greeting on her face with brush and ink. As with Venus de Milo in *Zed*, sex, books and money are again intimately intertwined, since Nagiko's family is supported by her father's homosexual publisher who takes his pleasure ritually on Nagiko's birthday: a sort of publisher's contract, if you will. The calligraphic face-painting ends on Nagiko's eighteenth birthday when she is persuaded into a disastrous marriage with the publisher's nephew. The marriage does not last long and Nagiko escapes to Hong Kong where she eventually becomes a successful fashion model. There she exchanges sex for calligraphy with her various lovers whom she encourages to write freely on every part of her body.

The pattern is broken when she meets a young English translator, Jerome, at the Cafe-Typo and he tells her she ought to try doing the writing for a change. Nagiko does indeed become a writer, but her first efforts are rejected by a publisher. Angered by this rebuff, she goes to see the publisher and is surprised not only to recognise her father's 'benefactor' from Kyoto but also to discover that his new lover is Jerome. Nagiko and Jerome in turn become lovers and he suggests that she write her text – promising thirteen erotic poems – on his body for presentation to the publisher. The publisher is delighted, as he is with subsequent calligraphic bodies sent to him by Nagiko. Jerome, in the meantime, is talked into faking a suicide to win back Nagiko's love. The fake turns out to be all too real and Nagiko is left with Jerome's corpse, which she decorates with

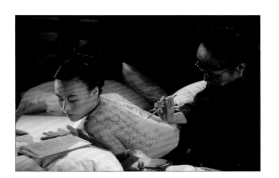

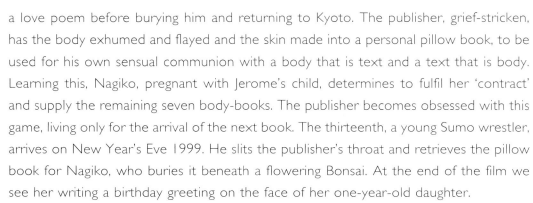

a love poem before burying him and returning to Kyoto. The publisher, grief-stricken, has the body exhumed and flayed and the skin made into a personal pillow book, to be used for his own sensual communion with a body that is text and a text that is body. Learning this, Nagiko, pregnant with Jerome's child, determines to fulfil her 'contract' and supply the remaining seven body-books. The publisher becomes obsessed with this game, living only for the arrival of the next book. The thirteenth, a young Sumo wrestler, arrives on New Year's Eve 1999. He slits the publisher's throat and retrieves the pillow book for Nagiko, who buries it beneath a flowering Bonsai. At the end of the film we see her writing a birthday greeting on the face of her one-year-old daughter.

We scarcely need to dwell on the Benjaminian resonances of the film's central conceit. The allegorised corpse of *The Pillow Book* seems to resume and encapsulate the entire baroque aesthetic of the earlier films, though it is significant that Jerome's body will not be left to rot on the ceiling: he is reduced to pure surface, his flesh, organs and even bones discarded; his body spiritualised by its transformation into text, the text sensualised by its perfect embodiment. The allegory, as with *The Draughtsman's Contract*, is a complex one (especially in terms of the way questions of race, gender and sexual orientation intersect here with familiar Greenaway themes of reproduction, transmission and redemption) and requires a kind of close, careful reading that space constraints will not permit here.

Drowning by Numbers

FROM ABOVE
sheep and tides; tug of war; beach cricket

OPPOSITE, L to R
The Audience of Mâcon

What interests us particularly, however, about this film is that it seems to participate as much in Greenaway's curatorial strategies, as they have been taking shape over recent years, as in the strategies of his filmmaking. In this sense, it is very close to *Prospero's Books* which, despite being an adaptation of Shakespeare, falls into the category of what we would call Greenaway's 'museum films' as opposed to his theatrical films like *The Draughtsman's Contract*, *The Cook, the Thief, His Wife and Her Lover*, and *The Baby of Mâcon*. (*A Zed & Two Noughts* and *Drowning by Numbers* would both be museum films, as would *The Belly of an Architect*, the only film to explore through its story the political economy of curating a major exhibition.) Clearly, such a sweeping binary has severe limitations and should not be seen as proposing some kind of hard and fast distinction between two kinds of film. There are elements of both genres in all the films, along with features of quite different genres altogether. However, if we understand that we are speaking here in terms of dominants rather than absolutes, the distinction can be useful in helping us to think through the relationship between filmmaking and curating in Greenaway's career.

So what do we mean by the term 'museum film'? We have in mind those films that, alongside the narrative or dramatic structure that pushes the action forward, explore alternative logics (and desires) – such as accumulation, saturation, seriality, taxonomy – in their representation of the world.[16] In these films, the syntagmatic (or metonymic) axis of plot and narrative (the axis of combination) tends to be disrupted by the paradigmatic axis of selection, foregrounded by various strategies of metaphor and display.[17] Thus, the thirteen calligraphic bodies of *The Pillow Book* are allowed to take on so much autonomy within the film's structure that we as audience run the risk of losing interest in the complicated story of love, death and revenge that ostensibly motivates their presence. Similarly, the catalogues of games and landscapes in *Drowning by Numbers* and the embodied books and tableaux vivants of *Prospero's Books* constantly distract our attention from whatever narrative pull these films might have and call for a more leisurely, contemplative form of spectatorship than is usually associated with the cinema.

In this respect, the ten projected exhibitions of the *Stairs* series reflect Greenaway's dissatisfaction with the inherent limitations of cinema and his desire to go beyond them: 'I am curious about the possibilities of taking cinema out of the cinema. I am curious about presenting cinema as a three-dimensional exhibition. I am curious about what constitutes a vocabulary of cinema. I am curious, I suppose, finally, in respect of the new technologies and the apparent morbidity of the old, how we are to go about reinventing cinema.'[18] His response has been to plan a series of ten investigative exhibitions to be held in ten different cities around the world, each exhibition exploring all the component elements of cinema but focusing on one dominant theme. Geneva, in 1994, took as its subject 'Location', while Munich in 1995 dealt with 'Projection'. 'Audience' will be examined in Lisbon in 1998 and after that it will be the turn of Acting, Properties, Frame, Text, Time, Scale and Illusion. (Audience had been the subject of *The Audience of Mâcon*, a 1993 exhibition of photographic costume portraits of film extras. The 1996 *In the Dark* installation at the Hayward Gallery, as part of its *Spellbound* exhibition on art and film, was an attempt to deal with four constitutive elements of cinema – acting, audience, properties and text. On a much larger scale, the *Cosmology at the Piazza del Popolo* exhibition in June 1996 allowed Greenaway and his lighting designer, Reinier van Brummelen, to transform one of Rome's busiest squares each evening with an extravaganza of light and sound recreating the history of the Piazza from Nero to Fellini.)[19]

What, then, are the limitations of contemporary cinema that Greenaway seeks to explore and redress through his exhibition strategies for *The Stairs*? The first is less intrinsic than historical and has to do with Greenaway's perception (shared by many) that the globalising tendencies of postmodern culture are also homogenising tendencies, producing a false universality which is little more than a rhetorical smokescreen for American dominance. The question here is how the local can be affirmed in a cinematic culture with a seemingly infinite capacity to recuperate and assimilate difference. A different kind of homogenisation is imposed by the persistence of the rectangular frame and its fixed aspect-ratio, the relationship of the vertical to the horizontal axis: 'Contemporary film-directors have at best three aspect-ratios to choose from – though the demands of television and its hold over the finances and therefore aesthetics of cinema threaten to reduce this to only one . . .'[20] Greenaway's recent work has been much con-

cerned with foregrounding and undermining this 'tyranny of the frame'.[21]

The third limitation is intrinsic to the medium and concerns the familiar problem of narrative when used in film instead of in books. Unlike the cinema-goer, the reader does not have to contend with the irresistible forward pull of the 24 frames a second of cinema and can therefore disrupt the narrative flow by putting the book down for a while, flipping back (or forward), or merely varying the pace of reading. Narrative in the cinema inevitably escapes the viewer's control and reinforces the power of the filmmaker to impose a particular vision and a particular experience: 'The contemplation of a viewer before a still image – a painting or a photograph – is dependent on the viewer's time-frame: the *Mona Lisa* can be viewed for four seconds or for four days. Cinema does not permit such space.'[22] According to Greenaway, the inexorable linearity of mainstream cinema, so closely tied to nineteenth-century concepts of narrative, might profitably be disrupted by the imaginative use of new electronic technologies that have the capacity to bring film narrative up to the levels of sophistication of a Joyce, a Borges or a Perec. However, as we saw in Chapter 4, Greenaway does not fall into the trap of technological determinism, remaining aware that the new media offer no guarantees that cinema can effectively be democratised and turned into a two-way traffic.[23]

The fourth limitation concerns audience and the possibilities offered by cinema for communion and community. We have already discussed this issue, but Greenaway has some interesting things to add in this new context: 'There has been not a little self-congratulation by film-makers on the special sociability of cinema, as though cinema might be offering a unique public-opportunity purgative for privately repressed emotions. But is a visit to the cinema really a community activity in the same way as going to the theatre or going to church or going to a football match? Or even as watching television in a small-audience domestic setting where speech is not banned, movement not restricted?'[24] Interestingly, when Greenaway muses about alternatives to the status quo, it is in rational, discursive terms more reminiscent of Brecht than Artaud. He dreams of a cinema with more social involvement, 'where the social activity is increased, where individual time-frames could be adjusted to the freedom of viewing, where there was a possibility for freedom of comparison of views, and no limit, within reason, of private conversation and discourse'.[25]

The fifth limitation has to do with cinema's lack of intrinsic materiality: 'Until the advent of the illusion-at-a-distance medium of film, all established cultural media had, and have, close association with corporeality and physicality, certainly with the corporeality of the creator and frequently with the corporeality of the audience.'[26] Film as substance gains nothing from age; exposed to the elements, it can only deteriorate. 'It gains no patina, no craquelure, makes no valuable chemical interaction with its environment.' As Benjamin would say, it has no aura: 'Every time you view a film, it is very predictably the same. It is interesting, and significant to this argument, that unlike a church or a house, a gallery or even a museum where other cultural artefacts are presented, the cinema where it shows means virtually nothing to the historical-cultural value of the film shown.'[27]

How does the *Stairs* project try to explore these limitations? For the Geneva exhibition, one hundred wooden, white-painted staircases were erected in different sites across the city to induce a sense of defamiliarisation and 'stair-consciousness'. Each staircase had a viewing platform and a viewfinder for the contemplation of a hundred fixed framings of the city, anchoring the exhibition firmly in the everyday life of the local with its ever-changing cast of actors and extras and endlessly variable weather and lighting conditions. 'Since the exhibition lasted a hundred days, it was credible that here were one hundred separate hundred-day long films with no film in the camera . . .'[28] One of the major concerns of the installation was with the act of framing, foregrounded and defamiliarised by constant variations in the aspect-ratio: 'thus notions of manufacturing a wide shot or a

BELOW and OPPOSITE
Stairs: Geneva

detail were possible without using either a wide-angle or a close-up lens, without pushing the landscape further from you, or bringing it artificially closer.'[29] Occasionally, the viewer's 'horizon of expectations' would be disturbed by framings based on a diagonal axis, thereby suppressing the 'comforting orthodox horizon' (and, incidentally, recalling the diagonal shots of the Victor Emmanuel Building during Kracklite's suicide scene).[30]

The installation originally planned for Barcelona in 1997 and then, after a change of circumstances, for Lisbon in 1998, will continue the exploration of the activity of the city as spectacle, but the focus will change slightly with the erection of a thousand numbered seats in various groupings at selected sites across the city. The intention is to 'create a hypothetical audience for a hundred days, to watch not spectacularly dramatized action, not pre-planned activity, but the everyday life of the city, as though it were a performance'.[31] Such an arrangement will encourage spectators to reflect on their own condition as audience, while potentially overcoming some of the intrinsic limitations placed on the traditional cinema audience (passivity, fixed time frame, lack of sociability and community). In Munich in 1995 the emphasis was different again, with spectators walking (rather than sitting) around a night-time city centre transformed and illuminated by the installation of a hundred screens (one for each year of cinema history) projected on the exterior walls of churches, museums, theatres and public buildings of all kinds.[32] This exhibition of cinema as 'a beam of projected light striking a surface with a framed rectangle of brightness into which shadows are introduced to simulate illusions of movement'[33] draws attention to the medium's lack of materiality by contrast with the all-too-solid structures of the architectural screens. At the same time, the projected image necessarily enters into new relationships with these screens which are not abstract, homogeneous and universal, but historically and materially rooted in the local.

The ambition of taking cinema out into the world might, at first sight, seem to run contrary to one of the main structuring principles of Greenaway's work as a whole – the obsession with collections of all kinds. Collecting, after all, is generally thought of as a strategy of containment, a quest for mastery that involves a denial of history and a withdrawal from the real world. According to Susan Stewart, '[t]he collection seeks a form of self-enclosure which is possible because of its ahistoricism. The collection replaces history with *classification*, with order beyond the realm of temporality. In the collection, time is not something to be restored to an origin; rather, all time is made simultaneous or synchronous within the collection's world'.[34] Collecting is an act of defunctionalisation and decontextualisation whereby the use value of an object is destroyed or totally aestheticised: the context of origin, the object's (everyday) life in time and place, is suppressed in favour of the synchronous logic or grammar of the collection. At the same time, the object experiences a loss of materiality as it becomes a mental construct, a cultural signifier defined in relation to a chain of other signifiers within the system.[35]

Jean Baudrillard has argued in this respect that collecting concerns only objects divested of their function and made relative to a subject: the system constituted by a collection is itself constitutive of the subject's world or personal microcosm; it is the means 'whereby the subject seeks to assert himself as an autonomous totality outside the world'.[36] The activity is particularly important in the case of the child, for whom collecting provides an early opportunity to exercise control over the outside world.

FROM ABOVE, L to R
Stairs: Munich

Drowning By Numbers

OPPOSITE, FROM ABOVE
*skipping girl and Smut; the hanged Smut; Smut
with cricket bat*

PAGE 94
Some Organising Principles

PAGE 95
Watching Water

(The tendency of the collecting impulse to disappear with the onset of puberty is humorously and poignantly dramatised in the remarkable figure of Smut in *Drowning by Numbers*, a film which, amongst other things, explores an anxious and ultimately unsuccessful passage from the closed world of childhood games to the realities of adult life.) For an adult, collecting fulfils an essentially escapist function, representing a retreat or regression to an unthreatened territory which one masters through arranging, ordering and classifying. In this sense, the collection is 'the ideal site of a neurotic equilibrium' in so far as 'it is invariably *oneself* that one collects': the final term of the succession is always the person of the collector.[37]

A collection, then, is a kind of synchronic haven, a translation of time into space, a refuge against the irreversible rush towards death: 'What man wants from objects is not the assurance that he can somehow outlive himself, but *the sense that from now on he can live out his life uninterruptedly and in a cyclical mode, and thereby symbolically transcend the realities of an existence before whose irreversibility and contingency he remains powerless.*'[38] Or, in Susan Stewart's terms, '[i]n the collection the threat of infinity is always met with the articulation of boundary' which allows it to function as a mode of control and containment: the contours of the self are constantly defined and confirmed by the generation of series.[39]

Stewart singles out the museum, with its claims to representativeness, as the privileged site of collecting in our culture. Building on an argument put forward by Eugenio Donato concerning the fiction promoted by the museum that its spatial disposition of fragments is capable of producing a coherent representation of the universe, Stewart concludes that 'there are two movements to the collection's gesture of standing for the world: first, the metonymic displacement of part for whole, item for context; and second, the invention of a classification scheme which will define space and time in such a way that the world is accounted for by the elements of the collection. We can see that what must be suppressed here is the privileging of the context of origin, for the elements of the collection are, in fact, already accounted for by the world'.[40] A special case is the natural history museum, which substitutes for the context of origin a spatial juxtaposition not occurring in nature but deriving rather from the articulations of the system of classification.[41] Similarly, Michel Foucault sees in the modern museum a heterotopia manifesting 'the will to enclose in one place all times, all epochs, all forms, all tastes, the idea of constituting a place of all times that is itself outside of time and inaccessible to its ravages, the project of organizing in this way a sort of perpetual and indefinite accumulation of time in an immobile place . . .'[42]

Is Greenaway, then, a collector in the sense described by Stewart and Baudrillard? Is he engaged, in his curatorial practices and 'museum films', in suppressing time and denying history? Does his work represent an attempt to control and contain the materiality of the world and its objects, to substitute system for process, order for anarchy? Are his experiments with series, taxonomies and catalogues merely a way of holding death at bay, of tracing the contours of an autonomous self outside the vicissitudes of history, the contingencies of everyday life? To argue along these lines would be to fall into the all too common trap of taking the representation for the thing itself. Yes, Greenaway's work is full of quirky collections and eccentric sets. Yes, the disruption of narrative by other, less temporal structures is a constant, as is the heterotopian urge to redistribute in space, according to new logics, objects taken from other times and other places. But, we would argue, these strategies are never employed naïvely. They are part of a critical exploration of collecting as a crucial aspect of our cultural behaviour.

The museum is never an innocent place in Greenaway's work and its relationship with the slaughterhouse is ever present. Next to the Willendorf Venus we see the decomposing corpse of a cow, alongside the letters of the alphabet a display of animal organs or human body parts. We are never allowed to forget that the museum, like architecture, is an instrument of social control, that its aesthetic redeployment of history is an (often bloody) strategy of power. Far from existing in a social vacuum, culture intersects with sex, money and death in a marketplace not only of ideas but of human lives and bodies; it is never disinterested but is bought and sold, contracted and traded in a constant struggle for possession and prestige, legitimation and authority. As for the structures themselves — the whacky compendiums, the self-deconstructing taxonomies — they are Greenaway's ironic way of turning the logic of the encyclopedia against itself. Ultimately, Greenaway's museum has only one exhibit: the corpse of culture dismembered and laid out for all to see, the endlessly recycled but always disconcerting allegory of a poor, bare, forked animal in all its mean nastiness and delightful invention. The naughty bits, we recall, are so very close to the dirty bits.

NOTES

1 Peter Greenaway, *A Zed & Two Noughts*, Faber and Faber, London, 1986, p36.

2 Venus de Milo not only tells (and sells) obscene stories about animals, she is also involved in negotiations with the zookeeper Van Hoyten, who offers animal parts in exchange for sexual favours. Later in the film, both Van Hoyten and Van Meegeren try, separately, to sell the body of the pregnant Milo to the Deuce brothers for use in their experiments on decomposition; the brothers settle for a pregnant Grevy's zebra.

3 Peter Greenaway, *Prospero's Books*, Chatto & Windus, London, 1991, p28.

4 *Ibid* pp20-21. The device of the poisonous book was used in Patrice Chéreau's 1994 film, *La Reine Margot*, and in Umberto Eco's novel *The Name of the Rose*.

5 *Ibid* p20.

6 *Ibid* p24.

7 *Ibid*.

8 Peter Greenaway, 'Introduction', *Hundert Objekte Zeigen die Welt/Hundred Objects to Represent the World*, Verlag Gerd Hatje, Stuttgart, 1992, no pagination.

9 That the exhibition's ordering principle was intended to be subversive of traditional museum culture hardly needs to be stressed: 'It was, on my choosing, to be an exhibition that placed art objects of so-called high cultural reputation with objects of low cultural standing, and with objects of apparently no cultural credentials at all; an exhibition whose taxonomy was subjectively subversive, having nothing in common with the five orthodox categories of taxonomy that museum culture generally sees as relevant — namely, the categories of age, authorship, nationality, material and ownership' (Peter Greenaway, *The Stairs/Geneva: The Location*, Merrell Holberton, London, 1994, p14).

10 The description is delightfully self-mocking: 'To demonstrate obsession, ornithology, hearing, flight, encyclopedic thoroughness.'

11 Cf the case of Samuel Pepys who, after many rearrangements of his library, settled on a classification according to size, thereby subordinating subject and reference convenience to a particular aspect of material condition. See Susan Stewart, *On Longing: Narratives of the Miniature, the Gigantic, the Souvenir, the Collection*, Johns Hopkins University Press, Baltimore, 1984, p155.

12 Object #82 represents the soul: a refrigerated display of animal organs on one side of the cabinet; on the other, 'some invented and (exquisitely) made organs that might well represent the "soul" if we could find it'.

13 *Prospero's Books*, p17.

14 On the different types of *mise en abyme*, see Lucien Dällenbach, *Le Récit spéculaire. Essai sur la mise en abyme*, Seuil, Paris, 1977. We should note that, to suggest infinite reduplication (or regression), it is sufficient to actually represent only two levels of the structure: the imagination will do the rest. Similarly, it is enough to exhibit only 100 objects to represent the world, since any individual can reconstitute, by association, the totality of her universe from a sufficiently varied (but limited) sample. The same principle is at play in *Drowning by Numbers*, where the Skipping Girl, who sets all the film's number games in motion, knows that it is enough to count the first 100 stars.

15 The twenty-fourth of Prospero's books is the 1623 edition of Shakespeare's plays, with the nineteen pages of *The Tempest* left blank.

16 In *The Stairs/Geneva: The Location*, Greenaway raises this perennial problem again, claiming that his 'experiments with numerical systems, alphabetical sequence, colour-coding, have all been attempts to dislodge this apparently unquestioned presumption that narrative is necessary and essential for cinema to convey its preoccupations' (pp12-13). This does not mean that either we or Greenaway accept the binary reductionism of much contemporary writing, which is far too quick to equate narrative with ideology and non-narrative with critique. On this, see Dana Polan, 'Brief Encounters: Mass Culture and the Evacuation of Sense' in Tania Modleski (ed), *Studies in Entertainment: Critical Approaches to Mass Culture*, Indiana University Press, Bloomington, 1986, pp167-87.

17 We say 'various strategies of metaphor and display' because Greenaway's exhibitions themselves are far from obeying the same principles of representation. We have seen, in *100 Objects*, a selection made of an arbitrarily fixed number of exhibits which are then imaginatively expanded by analogy to represent (exhaustively, encyclopedically) the world. The strategy of *Flying Out of This World*, an exhibition curated by Greenaway at the Louvre in 1992, would seem to have been almost the opposite, since there he selected a limited number of drawings from the Louvre's vast collection according to a principle of thematic saturation. A single semantic field, comprising the terms *flying*, *falling*, *lifting* and *gravity*, is saturated with illustrations, which are then unpacked metonymically to generate a series of mini-narratives. (The process recalls Baudelaire's anecdote about Balzac at the Exposition Universelle of 1855. Standing in front of a painting of a snowy winter landscape dotted with peasant cottages complete with smoking chimneys, the novelist can only muse aloud about what is happening *inside* the humble dwellings. Was the harvest good? Can they pay their rent? Baudelaire laughs but acknowledges that Balzac has a point and that often a painting is best appreciated by the number of ideas or daydreams to which it gives rise. It is exactly this kind of narrativisation of images that we see at work in the catalogue of the Louvre exhibition.)

18 *Peter Greenaway, The Stairs/Munich: Projection*, Merrell Holberton, London, 1995, p9. In *The Stairs/ Geneva: The Location*, he describes his project of exporting cinema language out of cinema and into the world as 'a sort of mega-cinema' (p9).

19 *A Times* report on the Piazza del Popolo exhibition enthuses that 'Romans are grateful that a British director has given them (if only for one week) the score, lights and setting for an outdoor Cinecitta' (Julia Owen, 'Romans in the Gloaming', *The Times*, June 1996, Arts Section, p40). Greenaway is quoted as complaining that the 100-year-old tradition of cinema is 'old and tired'. '"We talk about the future of multimedia, yet we still have the spectator sitting in his seat for two

hours at a time watching an old-fashioned two-dimensional image", he says, gazing at the short-sleeved spectators on a hot mid-summer night. "I do hate cinemas, don't you?'"

20 *The Stairs/Munich: Projection*, p19.

21 This is the title of a 1996 exhibition held at the Galerie Fortlaan in Ghent.

22 *The Stairs/Munich: Projection*, p21. Elsewhere, he argues that 'small-scale miniaturisation of a film at much reduced quality levels for personal-control video-viewing is by no means any sort of answer to this particular problem' (*The Stairs/Geneva: The Location*, p3).

23 *The Stairs/Munich: Projection*, pp21-22. As we have argued at length elsewhere, the use of technologies, like the use of procedures or techniques, must be judged on a case by case basis in full consciousness of the historical and social circumstances of their deployment. See Bridget Elliott and Anthony Purdy, 'Peter Greenaway and the Technologies of Representation: The Magician, the Surgeon, Their Art and Its Politics', 'Art & Film' *Art & Design*, profile 49, 1996, Academy Editions, London, pp16-23.

24 *The Stairs/Munich: Projection*, pp23-24.

25 *Ibid* p24.

26 *Ibid* p25.

27 *Ibid* p26.

28 The description ironically recalls Neville's vain attempts to keep the grounds of Compton Anstey free of human traffic. In *The Stairs* project in general, the anecdotal and incidental are foregrounded and promoted in the absence of any scripted plot.

29 *The Stairs/Munich: Projection*, p27 for this and the previous quotation.

30 *Ibid* p29.

31 *Ibid* p31.

32 The idea of a walking, talking, highly sociable audience had already been foregrounded as one of the chief advantages of the museum exhibitions over the enforced sedentary passivity of the cinema audience. See *The Stairs/Geneva: The Location*, p28.

33 *Ibid* p39.

34 Susan Stewart, *op cit* p151.

35 Benjamin's view of collecting varies in a number of respects from the one put forward by Susan Stewart, but it does insist on the defunctionalisation of the object. From this point of view, and bearing in mind our discussion of allegory in Chapters 1 and 2, one can readily understand why Benjamin sees the collector as an allegorist. As Michael P Steinberg explains, '[t]he collector is an allegorist, but his resulting patterns of meaning are capricious, scattered. The Benjaminian collector is not a taxonomist' ('The Collector as Allegorist: Goods, Gods, and the Objects of History' in Michael P Steinberg [ed], *Walter Benjamin and the Demands of History*, Cornell University Press, Ithaca, 1996, p115).

36 Jean Baudrillard, 'The System of Collecting' in John Elsner and Roger Cardinal [eds], *The Cultures of Collecting*, Harvard University Press, Cambridge, MA, 1994, p8.

37 *Ibid* pp11, 12.

38 *Ibid* p17. Original italics.

39 Susan Stewart, p159.

40 *Ibid* p162.

41 For an interesting account of how the kind of decontextualisation practised by museums constitutes a strategy of power linked to hegemonic capitalism, see Daniel J Sherman, 'Quatremère/Benjamin/Marx: Art Museums, Aura, and Commodity Fetishism' in Daniel J Sherman and Irit Rogoff (eds), *Museum Culture: Histories, Discourses, Spectacles*, Routledge, London, 1994, pp123-43.

42 Michel Foucault, 'Of Other Spaces', *Diacritics* 16/1, Spring 1986, p26.

OPEN TO INTERPRETATION
The Framer Framed

No one should be telling us that we need films to suit every taste. At this point, we are far beneath taste. Just the opposite is true: the crisis in films is not really based on an aesthetic level but on an intellectual one. Basically, films suffer from such obvious stupidity that aesthetic quarrels are relegated to the background.

André Bazin[1]

While Peter Greenaway might well agree with Bazin's remarks as quoted here by Truffaut, many of his critics would be horrified by what they would consider an unrepentantly elitist value judgement. It is perhaps not surprising that his films have been much better received in France, where there is a long tradition of artistic filmmaking, than in Great Britain. This chapter will take up the question of Greenaway's reception and discuss some of the more controversial issues surrounding his work.

If Greenaway's films are often characterised as obsessive, the same might be said of the criticism that addresses them. Since his first foray into feature filmmaking with the release of *The Draughtsman's Contract* in 1982, critics have tended to place Greenaway in a special category, echoing the director's repeated assertion that he is not a filmmaker, but rather a painter who works in cinema.[2] Critics writing for mass-market publications have anxiously warned potential viewers that Greenaway movies are 'like no other you've ever seen'.[3] While reminding us that Greenaway's work belongs to an alternative art-house tradition, such warnings also point (albeit obliquely) to some of the more divisive aspects of his filmmaking. Michael Owen sums things up when he observes that '[n]o filmmaker divides opinion more, or more fiercely than Greenaway whose dense and formally structured films draw accusations of intellectual exhibitionism, emotional bankruptcy and pretentious elitism while his followers see him as the most original cinematic craftsman at work today'.[4]

Stories of traumatised and enraged viewers booing his films, storming out of the theatre, throwing objects at the screen, hurling abuse at the director, and even attacking the projectionist, approach the status of urban legend as they are circulated by film reviewers.[5] Even Greenaway admits, '[e]ver since my first movies, I've found that maybe a third of the audience walks out. I was lucky if they stayed for one-third of the picture before doing so. Now they stay maybe a little longer'.[6] At the other end of the spectrum, enthusiasts claim Greenaway is the most exciting intelligence working in contemporary cinema and point to the fact that, despite working outside Hollywood and on very modest production budgets, he has become over the past fifteen years a recognised international auteur with major conferences and whole issues of film periodicals devoted to his œuvre. Both Greenaway and his critics note that his films have been better received in

Japan and Continental Europe (where a substantial amount of the production money has been raised) than in Britain and North America. In this respect, it is telling that a Paris-based firm (Dis Voir) has published more of his filmscripts and artwork (in English, French and bilingual editions) than any single English-language publisher.[7]

When interviewed, Greenaway stresses that he wants to make films on his own terms and tries to avoid being manipulated by audiences or tempted by the formulaic psychodramas of Hollywood with its star system of actors who are called on to use only a limited range of acting techniques. He feels his own aesthetic and intellectual objectives are antithetical to those of Hollywood and ironically describes a brief flirtation with American producers in the late eighties:

> I got involved in a project two years ago. I thought that they would never accept it but I wrote a very full treatment. They paid me generously. I thought, okay, this is where we part company, because now I write the script. They paid me generously. Then we started talking about casting and before I knew where I was they were insisting that all words of more than four syllables had to go, and all dark areas of ambiguity had to disappear. The more control I lost, the more interest I lost. I would like to continue to make my own movies without interference. I've been lucky so far thanks to some forthcoming European producers.[8]

Elsewhere Greenaway emphasises the tension between trying to develop the most innovative cinematic vocabulary possible and minimising production costs in order to retain control over his films.[9]

Although this emphatic rejection of Hollywood might seem perverse (or hypocritical, according to the take), it should be seen in the context of attitudes shared by a number of people associated with the British Film Institute during the 1980s. Those who wanted to develop a viable middle-ground between the extremes of subsidised experimental filmmaking and commercial entertainment found a champion in Peter Sainsbury, the head of the BFI production board. It was Sainsbury who made Greenaway's move into feature filmmaking possible by generously funding *The Draughtsman's Contract* and *A Zed & Two Noughts*. What the BFI was doing, according to him, was 'not so much providing a finishing school or a training course but more battling out a place for him in the world. In other words, driving a wedge into existing institutions to allow Greenaway to work'.[10] Rejecting what he felt was essentially a 1950s production paradigm, which saw Hollywood as the nirvana of the successful filmmaker, Sainsbury wanted to nurture an innovative and alternative form of commercially viable English/European filmmaking.

Since the mid-1980s, Kees Kasander, Peter Greenaway's Dutch producer, has been largely responsible for keeping this vision alive by raising production money from such diverse sources as Film Four in England, the Coproduction Fund for the Dutch Broadcasting Corporation, Elsevier Vendes Film, Prokino in Germany, BAC Films in France, and NHK, a leading Japanese television broadcasting company which donated much of the high-definition video equipment and technical support staff used in the post-production editing of *Prospero's Books*.[11] Kasander, a former producer of the Rotterdam Film Festival, shares Greenaway's conviction that it is time to reinvent cinema: 'Celluloid is so limited and so conventional nowadays, so badly organized – the large crews, the way it's shot, the cameras, so many problems, so stupid, so back-to-the-Middle-Ages – that it's time to leave all that behind and do something different.'[12] This 'something different' involves exploring controversial ideas, structuring meaning in unconventional ways, as well as utilising new technologies to achieve a complex layering of sight and sound. These are creative liberties that could not be accommodated in a Hollywood system devoted to maximising profits, as Kasander stresses when he notes that *The Cook* was made on a minimal budget of $2.3 million. Since such productions cannot compete financially with the big studios, all those involved must have more in mind than just money: 'Everyone who did this film did it because he or she wanted to do a Greenaway film.' For his part, Greenaway openly acknowledges the influence of his producer with his A and B principle of alternating ventures: 'I'm allowed to make a film that's a little more accessible, and if that works and the equation is moderately successful at the box office, I'm allowed to be a little more recherché.'[13]

Before we turn to some of the more thorny issues which polarise reviewers, it is useful to have some idea of how critical responses to Greenaway have evolved over the course of his seven feature films released since 1982.[14] As critics have seen progressively more of Greenaway's work, they have been able to identify a number of recurring thematic concerns, including the obsession with creativity and (re)production in both cultural and biological terms, the fascination with encyclopedic systems of knowledge, often undercut by events or played off against one another in ironic conflict, and the darkly comic view of human life as inevitably subject to death and decay. They have also come to expect certain signature traits: driving (often neo-baroque) scores by Michael Nyman and others, artificially exaggerated costumes and ornate settings from different historical periods, endless quotations from the visual arts, extensive use of overtly theatrical and self-referential devices, and playfully stylised dialogue. Since we do not have enough space to discuss each film's reception in detail, we shall look instead at three key moments in the criticism: Greenaway's welcome to the world of feature filmmaking on the release of *The Draughtsman's Contract*, reaction to the new directions signalled by *A Zed & Two Noughts*, and the scandal over the American X-rating of *The Cook*. As the critical discourse subsequent to *The Cook* has tended to settle into more predictable patterns, we shall address the more contentious aspects of Greenaway's work in a more general way, rather than analysing the response to individual films.

It is important to realise that Greenaway's conspicuously 'new' style of filmmaking seemed to hold endless promise in the case of *The Draughtsman's Contract*. Most critics were perfectly happy to welcome to the movie mainstream a filmmaker who had cut his teeth in the relative obscurity of experimental film. They saw Greenaway as the latest success in a New British Cinema which they associated with such diverse directors as Attenborough, Puttnam and Jarman.[15] With a few exceptions (for example, the *New Yorker* critic Pauline Kael), reviewers celebrated the film's 'Englishness' which they detected in the landscape and in the mixed genre of country-house murder mystery cum Restoration drama, as well as in the 'upstairs, downstairs' interaction of different social classes.[16] In fact, many saw the film as a successful revitalisation of older genres, an 'optimum balance between convention and idiosyncrasy' that provided a new and more sophisticated form of postmodern entertainment for the sort of English and Anglophile audiences that enjoyed Agatha Christie, *Brideshead Revisited* and other forms of '"high-quality", middle-brow theatre and television.'[17] Aside from Pauline Kael's observation that sex was portrayed as a source of power rather than pleasure, little was said about the representation of gender. Although the legacy of Greenaway's structuralist experience was acknowledged, the more critical and darkly absurdist aspects of his vision were downplayed or overlooked in the first wave of enthusiasm which greeted the film. While critics realised that the film was by no means a 'straight' historical drama, they were not quite sure who or what was being parodied or what the irony might mean.

Perhaps the accusation that Greenaway sheds fans like autumn leaves best applies to the case of his second feature film, *A Zed & Two Noughts*, released in 1986. Although certain later films such as *The Baby of Mâcon* have been even less popular with general audiences, they have neither changed direction as abruptly nor followed so closely on the heels of early success. According to Greenaway, the shift in *Zed* was deliberate: 'After my modest success a lot of people expected me to make *Son of Draughtsman's Contract*. I wasn't interested in doing that. I went off at a completely different tangent and tended largely to destroy a lot of the confidence people had with that film. Some people disliked *A Zed & Two Noughts*, but what it did was create a different kind of audience; and with the third film, *The Belly of an Architect*, the audience for the first two films could hopefully come together.'[18] Certainly, *Zed* polarised film critics sharply. Some complained the film was intellectually cold and absurdly pretentious in its engagement with 'big' ideas relating to art, science, religion and morality. Others felt that viewing the film was as exciting as 'being locked in a cocktail party with a horde of structuralists' or watching a 'retrospective devoted to television weather forecasts delivered over a 30-year period at 11 p.m. Eastern standard time'.[19] Most thought Greenaway had simply returned to the experimental concerns of earlier films such as *The Falls*. From this point on, those who disliked his work would repeatedly deride the arrogant intellectualism and emotional bankruptcy of his films, charges we will try to evaluate in a moment.

If it was *The Draughtsman's Contract* that established Greenaway's reputation in England and Europe, *The Cook, the Thief, His Wife and Her Lover* was the film that received most attention from North American audiences and critics. Much was made of the fact that Greenaway seemed to have abandoned his typically icy detachment to produce a violently passionate film which drew violently passionate responses, especially after the Motion Picture Association of America classified it as an X-rated (or pornographic) film. After an unsuccessful appeal, Greenaway's American distributor Miramax released the film without any classification. The issue was taken up by a number of leading film critics, including Caryn James of the *New York Times* who used the case to criticise the limitations of the rating system, a position that was quickly countered by neo-conservatives such as David Denby, who argued that *The Cook* was simply a form of '"stylized" sadism' masquerading as 'high-falutin art' that deliberately incited controversy in order to generate better distribution and box office returns.[20] If this last accusation were true, Greenaway would have to be more than a little disappointed in the lack of long-term success of this 'strategy' of cheap sensationalism, since the anxiety surrounding his films has more recently lost more audiences than it has attracted. Charges of violence and pornography resurfaced with a vengeance in the case of *The Baby of Mâcon* which, in North America, has been shown only at festivals and in private cinema clubs because distributors have

A Zed & Two Noughts

ABOVE and OPPOSITE, FROM L to R
*Peter Greenaway on the set; Siamese twins; Alba
in bed, framed by the twins; sleeping child*

been unwilling to touch it.[21] Once again a number of reviewers complained that Greenaway went to 'stomach-turning lengths with scenes of explicit sex and violence' that were worse than those perpetrated by the creators of *Friday the 13th* and *Nightmare on Elm Street* because they pretended to be art.[22]

The charge that Greenaway deliberately confuses art and pornography is the first of three contentious issues that we want to address here. A litany of complaints on this subject address, among other things, the seemingly gratuitous parades of nudity, the degradation of bodies and sexual acts, the obsession with death and decay, the sometimes scatological language, and the representation of shockingly unconventional and perverse forms of violence ranging from physical and emotional humiliation to cannibalism and dismemberment. Those critics who complain most strenuously about violence and pornography usually refuse the possibility of allegorical interpretation or critical distance on the part of either director or audience. Instead, some argue that violence and cruelty are literally celebrated, while others claim they are symptomatic of the director's sadistic desire to disempower his audience. The accusation that Greenaway's films offer a gratuitous celebration of violence is usually made by neo-conservatives such as David Denby, William Green or Bill Brownstein, who would like to see his work suppressed or, at the very least, distributed with cautionary warnings. According to these writers, representation necessarily entails advocacy.[23] The other tack – that Greenaway deliberately disempowers his viewers – has been taken by critics of varying political and ideological persuasions, ranging from Scott Malcomson's leftist critique of the politics of *The Draughtsman's Contract* to the self-professed liberalism of Pauline Kael, who flatly asserts

that '[t]he notion, suggested by several reviewers that this movie [*The Cook*] is some kind of political allegory is absurd'.[24] Speaking for many, Jeanne Silverthorne argues that the artificiality of Greenaway's films turns their violence into a senseless spectacle which denies any possibility of identifying with the characters and consequently any sense of moral responsibility: 'Brutalized, we are given no way to assimilate that brutality . . . The ascendancy of violence is part of the genre to which this film contributes.'[25]

The problem of completely collapsing the distance between representational and material practices has recently been discussed by Wendy Steiner, who advocates a liberal aesthetics in which art is understood as 'neither identical to reality nor isolated from it, but a virtual realm tied to the world by acts of interpretation'.[26] According to Steiner, both left and right-wing fundamentalists tend to read art literally, though for rather different reasons. On the one hand, the left tends to condemn traditional works of art claiming they perpetuate an existing system of sociopolitical inequality and privilege, while on the other, the right tends to attack controversial, innovative or avant-garde forms of expression, arguing they undermine time-honoured social values. We will take up the latter arguments first, because hitherto Greenaway's neo-conservative critics have been more shrill and more numerous. Arguing against neo-conservative prosecutions of work by photographic artists such as Robert Mapplethorpe and Sally Mann, Steiner notes that representations which raise the spectre of disturbing emotions (such as sadomasochism and child abuse) should not be automatically censored, since they may help us to examine our own feelings towards these issues. Steiner further notes that the genre of photography is particularly prone to prosecution because it has been considered the least artistic and most transparently documentary and easily reproducible art form.

Greenaway argues that filmmaking is equally restrictive since '[i]t is mimetic in essence, and because it is a photographic medium – and the camera can never lie – it is always enslaved for a large part to those erroneous ideas of truth that have dogged the still photograph'.[27] Furthermore, cinema is dominated by the realistic conventions of a Hollywood entertainment industry which tends to shy away from the sorts of provocative and dangerous ideas traditionally explored in European drama and novels.[28] Greenaway has always claimed he examines abusive behaviour, dangerous ideas and social taboos in a critical and socially responsible fashion. Rather than aestheticising or trivialising violence, he insists that the artificiality of his filmmaking deliberately directs the audience to read his films metaphorically as a set of limit-testing ideas. According to him, the more conventional violence of Hollywood is much more dangerous. The violence in *The Cook* 'wasn't a Donald Duck situation where he gets a brick on the back of the head and gets up and walks away in the next frame. This was violence that keeps Donald Duck in hospital for six months and creates a trauma which he'll remember for the rest of his life'.[29] A number of film critics have sympathised with Greenaway's position, stressing that his work places strenuous demands on the audience by asking us 'to witness our worst possible selves operating in the world, and then further ask[ing] us to consider what we would put in place to control that ominous operation'. Similarly, Gary Michael Dault insists that there is nothing erotic or much that is genuinely violent about the infamous rape scene in *The Baby of Mâcon* with its elaborately staged forest of 208 angry red phallic bowling pins, one of which is knocked over every time the girl is violated. Instead, Dault observes, '[t]his is a symbolic enactment, trucked out in the kind of pageantry that has more to do with literary passion than it does with pornography. You want real violence, go see *Reservoir Dogs* . . .'[30]

If conservative critics worry that Greenaway's films attack fundamental notions of social decency by dwelling on human evil and excess, a number of left-liberal critics complain about Greenaway's intellectual exhibitionism and cultural elitism. As we shall see, such charges are also based on overly literal readings of the films. We have already encountered Scott Malcomson's accusation that by defeating the upstart Neville, Greenaway effectively sides with the aristocracy in *The Draughtsman's Contract*. Other writers complain that Greenaway offers us a series of nostalgic visits to the great cultural artefacts of the past, which are 'about as exciting as a guided tour through an ancient museum where the catalogue has been lost'.[31] Pauline Kael goes further than most when, in discussing *The Cook*, she accuses Greenaway of being a cultural omnivore who chews with

his mouth open, allowing his audience to 'identify almost every piece of art that has fed his imagination'. Warming to her theme, Kael asserts that '[w]atching this picture is like being trapped in a nightmare art-history seminar; we sit there, cowed and miserable, as the teacher spews high-toned abstractions and dares us, smirkingly, to raise a common-sense objection – we know we'll be ridiculed if we do'. All of which leads her to conclude that Greenaway 'has made a movie whose object is to push us to the ground and kick art in our faces'.[32] Georgia Brown voices similar feelings when she complains that the films induce panic attacks, imprisoning the viewer in a gilded rococo cage: 'I can almost chart a physical reaction – the moment I'll start feeling suffocated and constricted (like I have to move my limbs or be immobilized forever). Greenaway, who wants to be on top of everything, imposes his sensibility like a salmon net, or a bell jar.'[33]

According to a number of critics, kicking art in the viewer's face is only one of Greenaway's many tactics of intellectual intimidation. Others include the densely layered historical plots and conceits, the extensive literary references and allusions, and the sustained exploration of philosophical ideas and systems of ordering. Because these things cannot be absorbed in a single viewing, Greenaway is usually cast as a disconcertingly professorial filmmaker. (Perhaps it is not surprising that certain interviewers comment with evident annoyance on the fact that Greenaway dresses like an Oxbridge don and actually speaks in perfect sentences.) Understanding the films necessarily involves 'studying' them, which is not an idea that appeals to everyone as Schlomo Schwartzberg points out: 'I think the animosity to the man and his films is the result of the effort his movies require on the part of the viewer (and in that regard critics can be as lazy as anyone else).'[34] Mixing genres, layering cultural references and disrupting narratives, Greenaway's films are neither predictably entertaining nor easily interpreted. The pleasure on offer is that of thinking critically about what is represented, all of which takes us back to the issue of anti-intellectualism.

Why has there been so much fuss over Greenaway's films? After all, he readily admits he is not working for the mainstream market and that his films will not suit every taste. He cannot force audiences to watch his films, so why is he accused of kicking art in their faces? And why is the spectre of the sadistic art historian tyrannising his seminar used to demonise the filmmaker? Does the representation of cultural artefacts made under privileged conditions necessarily mean that one condones the values of the society, social group or artist who originally made or commissioned the works? Is it any coincidence that such complaints about the representation of high culture occur at a time when, according to critics such as Wendy Steiner, 'the popular opinion of academics has sunk to new lows'?[35] In North America (and, one might add, in post-Thatcherite Britain), this anti-intellectualism can be attributed to a complex array of factors, including neo-conservative attacks on public spending, disappointed liberal hopes that the educational reforms of the 1960s and 70s would reduce social inequalities, the increasing specialisation of research in the humanities and other fields which often makes academic work seem inaccessible, divisive debates over political correctness within the academy and attacks on the so-called privilege of intellectual freedom and academic tenure, all of which have left many scholars feeling overworked, frustrated and besieged. In this increasingly fraught educational climate one wonders what it means for someone to make films that ask of the viewer the kind of cultural exposure and interest that is increasingly being dismissed as elitist, outmoded and insufficiently oriented towards the job market. Is this conservative nostalgia of the worst kind, which insists that only an elite can enjoy such rare forms of cultural privilege? Or is there another way of understanding Greenaway's representation of cultural artefacts?

As we have tried to show in previous chapters, when one examines the rest of Greenaway's œuvre, the charge that he deliberately disempowers his audiences rings rather hollow. As our discussion of the *Stairs* project in Chapter 5 reveals, Greenaway wants to take cinema out into a world where audiences will actively participate in the event and break the spell of the cinematic spectacle. Giving his audience conceptual manoeuvring room is a crucial component of Greenaway's critical vision. Usually described as left-liberal in his political convictions, Greenaway seems determined to address issues of cultural authority.[36] His feature films have persistently explored who is responsible for making and controlling the dominant cultural values and representations in any given society: one could cite, by way of example, the analysis of property and landscape art in *The Draughtsman's Contract*, the investigation of systems of knowledge and power in *Prospero's Books*, as well as the uncomfortable juxtaposition of high culture and consumer greed in *The Cook* or the commodification of religion in *The Baby of Mâcon*.

Perhaps Greenaway comes closest to tipping his hand in *The Belly of an Architect* which has been read as a comment on the culture industry in general and, more particularly, on the role of the filmmaker in the spectacular world of late twentieth-century consumer capitalism.[37] In *The Belly*, art is not something removed from everyday life that a director can kick in our faces; it is a commodity that can be bought, sold and traded like any other. As Coco Fusco argues, 'Greenaway's film is an allegory about the inevitable incorporation of cultural products into the manipulations of mass culture [. . .] Stressing the futility of the search for origins or the resurrection of artistic heroes, Greenaway realistically emphasizes the necessity of coming to terms with popular culture and technological reproducibility'.[38] Thus we are confronted with a position that is more pragmatic than nostalgic. The representation of cultural artefacts made under privileged social conditions in the past does not mean that those conditions are necessarily endorsed, or that those artefacts enjoy a rarefied existence in some hypothetical aesthetic sphere. Like everything else, they participate in the late twentieth-century cultural marketplace. Once again, we realise that representation does not necessarily entail advocacy. Filmmakers (and even art historians) can critically interrogate the privileged category of art without ceasing to enjoy the objects produced in its name.

In the final analysis, it is this sort of aesthetic pragmatism that distinguishes Greenaway's use of allegory from that of earlier writers such as Walter Benjamin. The corruption, decay, death and dismemberment in Greenaway's films do not point to some sort of spiritual regeneration or transcendence as they do in the case of Benjamin's analysis of seventeenth-century German tragic drama. Time and again, Greenaway's critics lament the fact that his cinema offers little in the way of consolation or redemptive vision. In fact, there is an explicit rejection of religious experience and sentimental humanism alike, and no grand narrative of progress or self-realisation, whether Christian, Hegelian, Marxist or Freudian. In the end, the only certainty is death and decomposition. But that is also the beginning. Describing his own black sense of humour, Greenaway observes, 'I think our attempts to make life tragical tend to the pretentious and bombastic, and my purpose is to show instead that life is short, sharp, bizarre and farcical. I suspect that sometimes people don't know how to take the humour'.[39]

Evidently, many film critics find such messages unpalatable. Lamenting the fact that, until *Prospero's Books*, Greenaway had been locked into a deconstructive mode, with each film calling into question the very activity that brought it into existence, Vernon Gras at last detects something more positive in Greenaway's Shakespearean adaptation, where love overcomes hatred, forgiveness triumphs over revenge, benevolence over egotism, knowledge over ignorance, and orderly succession over usurpation. But sadly, this tiny spark of optimism fizzles out with *The Baby of Mâcon*, in which Greenaway returns yet again to themes of greed and perversion, leading Gras to complain: 'We find no balm in Greenaway, no possible alternative vision. His films remain agnostic, even nihilistic about any possible cultural improvement, while they continue scathingly to censure our animal rapacity to "fuck things up" . . . One cannot remain fixated on self-doubt and register the same note continually like an organ with a faulty stop unless one little cares whether the audience is still listening.'[40] For Greenaway, such moralising recriminations can scarcely be taken seriously in a world where 'the good are seldom rewarded, the bad go largely unpunished and the innocent are always abused'.[41] One has only to think of the ends met by Neville, Madgett, Michael, Jerome, the miracle baby and his sister to realise that, in Greenaway's world, the workings of justice, whether human or divine, are obscure to say the least.

The last word on these matters belongs to Geoffrey Braithwaite, whose admirable common sense might serve as a model to us all. After outlining the 'case against' Flaubert and defending the writer against charges, amongst others, that he hated humanity, that he did not believe in progress, that he was not interested enough in politics, that he did not involve himself in life, that he was a pessimist, that he taught no positive virtues, that he was a Sadist, and that there were a lot of animals slaughtered in his books, the good doctor came to the most damning accusation of all: that he believed in Beauty. A tricky charge to handle in fundamentalist times, but Braithwaite is up to it; subtle and nuanced in argument, forthright and unequivocal as ever, his response is crystal clear: 'I think I've got something lodged in my ear. Probably a bit of wax. Just give me a moment to grip my nose and blow out through my eardrums.'[42] And what was that you were saying about Greenaway? Ah. We begin to see what you mean. Just give us a moment to . . .

NOTES

1 Quoted in François Truffaut's introduction to André Bazin, *The Cinema of Cruelty*, (trans) Sabine d'Estrée, Seaver Books (New York), 1982, pxi. Truffaut notes that, from the time of his first articles until the end of his career, Bazin called for a more mature and responsible cinema.

2 See Greenaway's discussion of this in Gavin Smith, 'Food for Thought', *Film Comment* 26/3, June 1990, pp57, 60.

3 Jack Kroll, 'In the Eye of the Beholder', *Newsweek*, July 4, 1983, p78.

4 Michael Owen, 'Filming by Numbers', *Evening Standard*, August 23, 1991, p22.

5 See, for example, recent descriptions of Greenaway's audiences in John Walsh, 'A Shock to the System', *The Independent Magazine*, September 11, 1993, p18; Ken Shulman, 'Peter Greenaway Defends his "Baby"', *New York Times*, February 6, 1994, p18; Gary Michael Dault, 'The Baby, the Virgin, the Gore and the Bowling Pins', *Eye Weekly*, Toronto, September 16, 1993, p26. Such accounts also recall the audience brawls around Dada or the legendary première of Jarry's *Ubu Roi*.

6 John Walsh, p18. In an interview with Brian McFarlene in *Cinema Papers* 78, March 1990, p69, Greenaway describes the *succès de scandale* surrounding *The Cook* which apparently surprised him: 'There are people throwing coke bottles at the screen and threatening to burn down the cinemas; women are running out into the street to vomit. This is extraordinary, excitable behaviour for this comparatively modest little film to engender.'

7 The first claim is made by Sean French, 'Spit Roast: The Cook, the Thief, His Wife and Her Lover', *Sight & Sound* 58/4, Autumn 1989, p278, while Thomas Elsaesser describes Greenaway's status as an international auteur as a mixed blessing in 'Games of Love and Death or an Englishman's Guide to the Galaxy', *Monthly Film Bulletin*, October 1988, p290. The French journal *Cahiers du Cinéma* devoted a seminar to *The Draughtsman's Contract* which is discussed in Alan Franks, 'Camera Obscura', *Times Saturday Review*, August 24, 1991, p10, and *L'Avant-Scène Cinéma* 417/418, December 1992/January 1993 is entirely devoted to Greenaway's work. It should be noted that the British firm of Faber and Faber published the filmscripts for *A Zed & Two Noughts*, *Drowning by Numbers* and *The Belly of an Architect*, while *Prospero's Books* appeared with Chatto & Windus and Merrell Holberton put out the exhibition catalogues for the Geneva and Munich installments of *The Stairs*. Dis Voir has published scripts for *The Falls*, *Rosa*, *The Cook, the Thief, His Wife and Her Lover*, and *The Baby of Mâcon*, as well as a book of drawings and paintings entitled *Papers/Papiers*, a bilingual text around *Drowning by Numbers*, and a multi-authored book on Greenaway in French.

8 Ronald Bergan, 'Food for Thought', *Films & Filming*, October 1989, p29. In an interview with John Walsh (p20), Greenaway describes another encounter with two American producers which seems more like an absurd event from one of his films than a serious business proposition. 'They asked me to pursue certain ideas . . . and I did look at a certain Canadian novel, the money was interesting, my vanity was touched. I produced a script I thought they couldn't possibly be interested in because it was more a Greenaway project than the original; but they were. So we went into casting. They wanted Jane Fonda to play a 15 year-old soprano – well there was no question of that – all words of more than three syllables had to come out. They said, No water images Mr Greenaway, no flying, certainly no nudity . . . They tried to sue me when I backed out.' Still on the subject of Hollywood filmmaking, see Greenaway's comments to Gavin Smith, pp59-60, where he asserts that *The Cook* was a film that could never have been made in America, and to Robert Enright, 'The Rational Extremist: An Interview with Peter Greenaway', *Border Crossings*, 1990, p79.

9 Roger Ebert, 'Director works "magick" with Bard in "Books"', *Chicago Sun-Times*, November 24, 1991.

10 Robert Brown, 'From a View to a Death [an interview with Peter Greenaway and Peter Sainsbury]', *Monthly Film Bulletin* 49/586, 1982, pp255-56.

11 See Greenaway's discussion of funding in Marcia Pally, 'Cinema as the Total Art Form: An Interview with Peter Greenaway', *Cineaste* 18/3, 1991, p10.

12 Howard A Rodman, 'Anatomy of a Wizard', *American Film*, November/December 1991, p27.

13 The first quote is from Terry Trucco, 'The Man Will Eat Literally Anything', *New York Times*, April 1, 1990 and the second from John Walsh, p22. Elsewhere Greenaway points out that Kasander has an amazing ability to cobble money together from various sources and stretch it so that he can make very rich, professional-looking movies on tiny budgets (McFarlene, p42).

14 At the time of writing, Greenaway's eighth feature film, *The Pillow Book*, is being premiered at film festivals. Since reviews are only just starting to appear, it has not been included in this discussion.

15 Greenaway's relationship to other English directors is raised in Karen Jaehne, 'The Draughtsman's Contract: An Interview with Peter Greenaway', *Cineaste* 13/2, 1984, p13. In this interview, as in many others, Greenaway admits that while many of his preoccupations are curiously English, he is not associated with the predominantly realist English tradition of filmmaking. He repeatedly asserts that he has been more influenced by a European tradition of cinema which would include Bergman's *The Seventh Seal*, Resnais's *Last Year in Marienbad*, Eric Rohmer's *Marquise von O* and Fellini's *Casanova*. See also Brian McFarlene, p69, for a slightly later discussion of his relationship to other British filmmakers. A more complex analysis of the New British Cinema is provided in Peter Wollen, 'The Last New Wave: Modernism in British Films of the Thatcher Era' in Lester Friedman (ed), *Fires Were Started: British Cinema and Thatcherism*, University of Minnesota Press (Minneapolis), 1993, pp35-51.

16 See Pauline Kael, 'Framed', *New Yorker*, August 22, 1983, p76, where she observes that '[t]here must be junkies for English upper-class movies (just as there are Nazi movie junkies): people who want to see over and over again the gardens, the halls, the finery, and the politesse, and, of course, the poisonous, warped behaviour'. Interestingly, writing several years later, the experimental filmmaker and critic Peter Wollen also recalls being 'nauseated by the excess of Englishness' when he first encountered the film at the Edinburgh Film Festival (Wollen, p46).

17 The first quote is from Tony Rayns, 'Peter Greenaway', *American Cinematographer* 64/9, September 1983, p46, and the second from Robert Brown, 'The Draughtsman's Contract', *Monthly Film Bulletin* 49, November 1982, p255. The reference to *Brideshead Revisited* appears in Mary Blume, 'A Public Triumph for a Private Movie', *International Herald Tribune*, December 31, 1982, p7.

18 The comment about shedding fans appears in Walsh, p18, as does Greenaway's description of the response to *Zed* (Walsh, p22).

19 The first quote is from David Edelstein, 'Rotters A Dog by Any Other Name', *Village Voice*, September 30, 1986, and the second from Vincent Canby, 'A Zed & Two Noughts', *New York Times*, September 20, 1986.

20 David Denby condemns James's position in 'Digestive Tract', *New York*, May 7, 1990, pp66, 68. Denby notes that although Hollywood movies were hurt by X-ratings, they contributed to the success of art house films like *The Cook* which, instead of premiering only in New York and Los Angeles, opened in eight American cities and was eventually distributed to over forty (but less than a hundred) theatres.

21 Schulman (p18) notes that, after being shown at Cannes, *The Baby of Mâcon* was purchased by distributors in twenty-seven countries, but not in North America.

22 Bill Brownstein, 'Greenaway's *Baby of Mâcon* is Trash Masquerading as Art', *The Gazette*, Montreal, July 8, 1994, pC3.

23 See, for example, William Green, 'One Man's Meat', *Sunday Telegraph Magazine*, October 1, 1989, pp16-17: 'But I wonder if anything much other than surface gloss distinguishes this work from the chainsaw hysterics and gutbucket horrors that your local video shop keeps on the top shelf? What are we to make of highbrow sex and violence? Is it easier to swallow if it is served up with an aesthetic dressing of Michael Nyman music and Sacha Vierny lighting? *The Cook, the Thief, His Wife and Her Lover* is in for a succès de scandale, and is sure to pack them in at art house cinemas this autumn. But I don't think audiences will be after food for thought. They will be there for a cheap thrill.'

24 Scott Malcomson argues that the unpleasantness of the aristocracy forces viewers to identify with Neville whose death ends up placing them in the same position of inferiority and subservience. See Scott Malcomson, 'The Draughtsman's Contract', *Film Quarterly*, Winter 1983-84, pp34-40; Pauline Kael, 'Conspicuous Consumer', *New Yorker*, May 8, 1990, pp88-90.

25 Jeanne Silverthorne, 'The Cook, the Thief, His Wife and Her Lover', *Artforum*, April 1990, pp23-24.

26 Wendy Steiner, *The Scandal of Pleasure: Art in an Age of Fundamentalism*, University of Chicago Press, Chicago, 1995, pp8, 36-40.

27 Peter Greenaway, *The Stairs/Geneva: The Location*, Merrell Holberton, London, 1994, p1.

28 See, for example, Greenaway's discussion of the differences between drama and film in Dylan Tran, 'The Book, the Theater, the Film and Peter Greenaway', *High Performance*, Winter 1991, p25.

29 Greenaway makes essentially the same point when discussing *The Baby of Mâcon*, noting that it 'is not a gore-splatter movie. [. . .] This is not a cartoon, Donald Duck-Bruce Willis situation. The film doesn't use violence as an instrument of pleasure. Here there is real retribution and real hurt. Here there is cause and effect'. See Ken Shulman, *op cit* p18.

30 Enright, *op cit* pp77-78, and Dault, *op cit* p26.

31 Adam Barker, 'A Tale of Two Magicians', *Sight and Sound*, May 1991, p27.

32 Pauline Kael, 'Conspicuous Consumer', *New Yorker*, May 8, 1990, pp88-90.

33 Georgia Brown, 'Prospero's Books', *Village Voice*, November 26, 1991.

34 Shlomo Schwartzberg, 'Acknowledging Greenaway', *Toronto Magazine*, October 21, 1991.

35 Steiner, *op cit* p153.

36 Tony Rayns, for example, describes Peter Greenaway as a left-liberal in 'Drowning by Numbers', *Monthly Film Bulletin* 55/657, October 1988, p290.

37 Greenaway returns to this issue in his *Stairs* project, where he notes: 'Perhaps more than any other medium, cinema is essentially circumscribed by technological parameters and by economic circumstances. For example, there are severe limits on choice of frame-aspect-ratio, and the length of a film is largely fixed by the desire of cinema managers demanding three performances a day to satisfy maximum audience attendance' (*The Stairs/Geneva: The Location*, p1).

38 Coco Fusco, 'Requiem for an Architect', *Art in America*, February 1988, p35.

39 Greenaway, cited in *The Listener*, August 1988, pp29-30.

40 Vernon Gras, 'Dramatizing the Failure to Jump the Culture/Nature Gap: The Films of Peter Greenaway', *New Literary History* 26, 1995, p142.

41 Peter Greenaway, cited in Rayns, *op cit* p289.

42 Julian Barnes, *Flaubert's Parrot*, Picador (London), 1985, p135. The whole of Chapter 10, 'The Case Against', makes wonderful reading for anyone interested in Greenaway.

COSMOLOGY

Rome, June 1996

The Cosmology at the Piazza del Popolo, Rome, in June 1996 was an exhibition which provided Greenaway and his lighting designer, Reinier van Brummelen, with the opportunity to transform one of Rome's busiest squares each evening of the month into an extravaganza of light and sound, recreating the history of the Piazza from Nero to Fellini

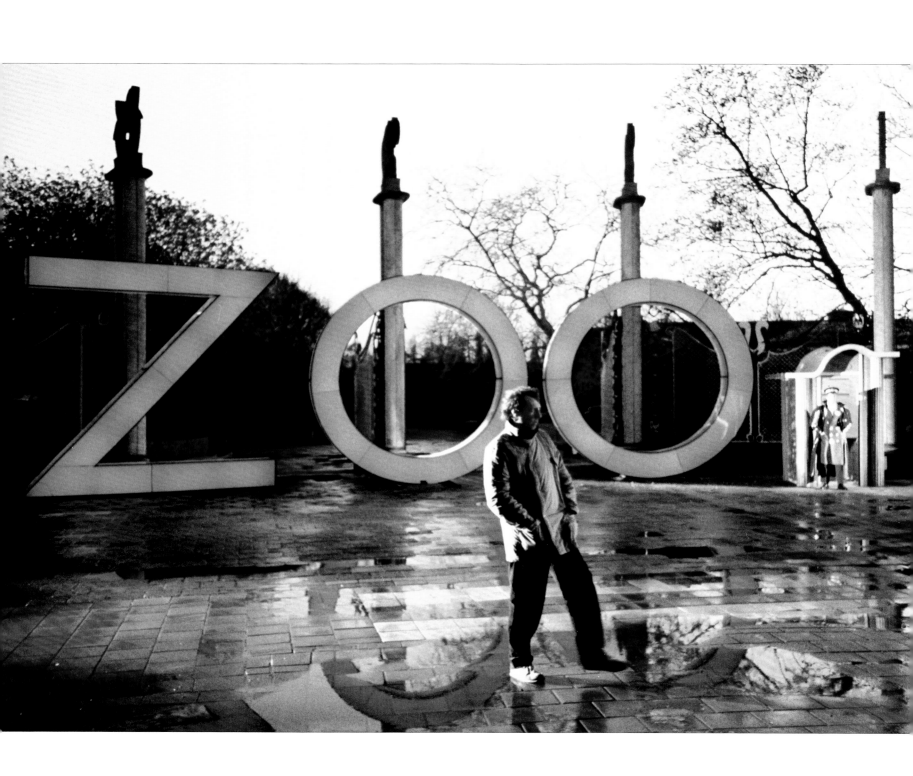

Peter Greenaway in front of the neon-lit ZOO

AN INTERVIEW WITH PETER GREENAWAY

Bridget Elliott and Anthony Purdy

Peter Greenaway received us at The VUE, tucked away behind a red door at the end of an alley in Hammersmith, London, on the afternoon of October 7, 1996. After a general chat, he offered the observation that, since our book was already finished, the interview might seem rather like a post mortem. For a variety of reasons, not least of which is the difficulty of sustaining 'death of the author' theories when faced with a very lively Greenaway, we prefer to think of it as a post scriptum. Reproduced here are a number of reflections drawn from a longer conversation. Our thanks to Peter Greenaway for a very pleasant afternoon, to Eliza Poklewski Koziell for her warm welcome at The VUE, and to Zoë Purdy for her help in transcribing the tapes.

You must be a pretty avid museum goer.
But not necessarily academic museums. If you regard a cathedral as a museum or if you regard a zoo as a museum, I would certainly try to visit those sorts of collections as well as the more orthodox institutions.

What do you look for when you go to a museum?
Principles of collection, principles of collation, the way things are organised. I would look for presentation as well as individual objects, because the medium in which objects and ideas are presented, as well as the museum's history and background, are significant for the way in which you appreciate the objects in it. You know there's a general feeling that museums are supposed to be neutral places. I don't think any museum in the world really can be that, no matter how hard it strives. Certainly in my curatorial activity, I might go to the opposite end and say, 'Look, this is a very subjective view of a particular situation, number of objects, ideas . . .' So far my curatorial projects have been temporary, so six months later somebody else can come along to those selfsame objects and reorganise them in a completely different way. But I do think, almost as a necessary political confession, we must say that museums are deeply subjective, based upon nationalism, particular ways of spending money, guilt at privilege, rapaciousness, competition among academics, and the continuing attitudes, political positions, idiosyncrasies, fashions and opinions of all the curators who've been responsible for putting the collections together. And we should include the architects and designers, too . . . the architect is important in shaping how collections are perceived.

Do you ever feel like an exhibition piece yourself or are you fairly philosophical about all the attention?

I have always felt my job as a filmmaker should extend after the projector has shut down. Since I hope I pursue a cinema of ideas, and the ideas are always more interesting than the films, I want to continue to talk about the ideas, so in that sense I'm all for the exposure. But sometimes I would agree that the artist really ought to go into total hibernation and not even show his face. But then the opposite point of view can also be canvassed. Certainly my distributors ask to see the face behind the work. But there's still a way in which I've sometimes wondered whether the author is necessarily the best person to talk to about his or her own work. In England, I have, in some quarters, been judged as elitist, bombastic, a cultural exhibitionist with a reputation for being mannerist and eclectic and confrontationalist in my own public defence. Foreign audiences seem to be more intrigued than audiences at home, and certainly the audience abroad is much larger. I'm a marginal UK figure. Perhaps if I could start again, I should be a filmmaker without an extra-film voice.

Because of some of the subject-matter and imagery in my films, when I walk through the arrivals-hall in a foreign airport, the meeting party sometimes seems to expect a Sadean, cadaverous figure who perhaps carries a coffin and rotting body parts in his luggage, and when they see the orthodox English bourgeois, with all the usual associations, their faces fall.

Where is the *Stairs* project right now? Is Barcelona going ahead?
There's been a Spanish election and a change of government and art funding can depend, as Christo discovered, on who's in power. So plans have changed and we will be making an exhibition in Barcelona called *Flying Over Water*, on the subject of the Icarus myth — with an eye on flying pioneers from Montgolfier, the Wright Brothers, Bleriot, Amy Johnson, to Gagarin. Plans were very seriously discussed to stage the next exhibition of *The Stairs* in association with the Lisbon Trade Expo 98, and to consider at the same time an exhibition on the Lisbon Earthquake. One of the most exciting characteristics for me about the staging of city-wide exhibitions, that I suppose Christo must have learned many years ago, is that it's a grand, public exercise in social persuasion. And this can be more important, indeed, than any aesthetic preoccupations. I've just returned from Israel, where there is enthusiasm for placing an exhibition of *The Stairs* in Jerusalem, an exhibition about touch and feel and body sensation of height, vertigo and gravity. We discussed the possibility of erecting one hundred tall towers all over the city.

But the territorial, political and religious problems are formidable, to say the least. Every yard of turf is foreign territory to someone with a very strong vested interest. Perhaps this very difficulty is the reason to do it.

Is Christo a particular inspiration for you?

A lot of the other Land Artists were a much greater influence – James Turrell and the Boyle Family in England still stand out – but of the 60s collection of Land Artists, I suppose it's Christo who is still very publicly flying the flag. I guess his persistent megalomania is also always attractive.

You have a very obvious interest in architecture. It functions, for example, as a master metaphor in *Belly*. But there's relatively little contemporary architecture foregrounded in your films. Is there a reason for that?

Well, you've just seen *The Pillow Book*. Renzo Piano's airport at Kansai is featured, very noisily, and he prided himself on its being a very quiet airport. Pei's Bank of China and Foster's Hongkong and Shanghai Bank are in the background of some very early shots. I suppose the creation, which was a collaboration with my design team, of that yacht-like building in *Drowning By Numbers* might be of interest as a foregrounded modern building. We sent the plans on request to a Belgian builder. There isn't much opportunity or scope to use modern architecture in seventeenth-century films that feature the Baroque. These movies had also become more and more interior, more and more claustrophobic, more and more designed as an artifice in the studio. So I suppose the last time we were out and about in the known world would have been with *Drowning By Numbers*, but there are certainly various parts in *The Pillow Book* where we are out and about. But to go on to our next project – *The Tulse Luper Suitcase* – we intend to revisit favourite architectural sites around the world, and some of those indeed will be modern buildings. I gave a lecture recently at the Architectural Association in London about my formal or professional connections with architecture – that had to demonstrate such a background was entirely bogus. I have no training as an architect, though I have been asked to judge architectural competitions, including a recent Estonian one for an expensive post-office complex.

You had Nigel Coates on the set of *The Draughtsman's Contract*. What was he doing there?

I wanted somebody else, since my job was to direct the film and worry about the committal of script to celluloid, to do the drawings, and we asked him; but his drawings turned out to be inappropriate and, in the end, I made them myself. I always believe it has to be the communicator's fault and not the communicatee's, so it must be my problem. But the need for veracity is part of the essence of that film. The draughtsman has a fetish to put down exactly what he sees. So it's a film about 'I draw what I see, not what I know'. And Nigel drew what he knew, not what he saw.

Amongst working architects, contemporary architects, which ones do you like?

Forgive the patriotism, but I support the English. I prefer Rogers to Foster, though I don't know what that tells you. Farrell I've always enjoyed. Despite the complaints about his two buildings on the Thames, I enjoy their strong symmetry and use of site. I also enjoy Nouvel and much new French architecture, and I'm very interested in architects from the Middle and Far East. My enthusiasms are eclectic. The Portland Building – the first project I had come across and understood as bringing a postmodern metaphor into architecture. And I think that Graves, in some senses, was the hidden model for Stourley Kracklite in *The Belly of an Architect*.

Any interest in the deconstructionists?

My background and interests are classical, with the stream of verticals and horizontals as masterplan, with the grid as a dominant twentieth-century painting proposition in the centre of the frame. My sympathies – sentimentally, nostalgically, intellectually and emotionally – would always go towards the notion of the classical form, the Apollonian universe, the continuing tradition in painting of della Francesca, Poussin, Mondrian, Jasper Johns, Sol Lewitt.

There's a lot of talk about the public responsibility of the architect, but what about the public responsibility of the filmmaker? Or of the curator of an exhibition?

With painting and filmmaking I think it's legitimate now to be governed and regulated by personal desire and taste, to acknowledge that a sense of responsibility must be my own seriousness of intent. I cannot think that Bacon and Picasso painted for anyone but themselves. It's still regarded as an act of arrogance to admit, as a filmmaker, that I must make films for myself. For me, it is arrogant to imagine I could make films for anyone else, especially since every member of the audience will want something different.

How do you respond to those charges of elitism when they come?

The six traditional art forms in the West have always been predominantly elitist. The study and practice of art have demanded education, specialist concentration and moneyed patronage; these things do not come easy or for free or without study. Cultural history repeatedly demonstrates that cultural artefacts that are valued are made for an elitist client or community or audience, whose interests are catered for with the collusion of the creator.

But appreciating the object doesn't necessarily mean embracing the kind of elitist structures that produced it.

Not at all. But perhaps we should not baulk at the word 'elitism'. Conceivably everyone is elitist in some occupation or interest. It's like that unfortunate use of the word 'mannerist' which was so inappropriately attached to a certain period of very exciting work between the Renaissance and the Baroque and which has taken people down the wrong path because of the pejorative connotations of the particular adjective. 'Elitism' does not have to be pejorative.

Which leads us back to questions of reception and your notion of alternating A and B films. We were particularly surprised by the North American reaction to *The Baby of Mâcon*.

I think it was a very important movie for me. And certainly I proselytised it to the hilt, more so than I've done any other movie.

Why did you need to? What happened with that film? Why did people try to shut it down and just not want it to be seen?
I think there are several reasons. First of all, the moral climate had changed. We were right in the middle of PC by the time *The Baby of Mâcon* came out, which I don't think was quite the situation with *The Cook, the Thief*. But maybe even more importantly, there was a great sense of irony about *The Cook, the Thief* which let people off the hook. There was a way in which its propositions were deliberately ludic, and melodramatic in a way people could understand. But *The Baby of Mâcon* for me was stripped of that particular sense of irony. It had some very serious propositions – exploitation of children, humiliation of women, blasphemy against the Roman Catholic Church, and, if you are an animal lover, the savaging of animals – items, not surprisingly, of considerable antagonism from most people's perspective. I would like to think that the most powerful thing about *The Baby of Mâcon* was its idea of 'audience' – cinema audience, theatrical audience, audiences in general – and the obsession with voyeuristic sex, violence and sensation at the end of the twentieth century. It was intended, in part, as a comment on contemporary voyeurism.

It's surprising to hear you talk of the lack of irony in *The Baby of Mâcon*, because to us it seems like a highly ironic film in its use of devices like the Masterpiece Theatre music.
The film is a costume drama. It is a self-conscious, ironic exposition of a cliched movie genre. The characters are forever ostentatiously taking their clothes on and off. And it is based on grandiose, grandiloquent conventions of the big nineteenth-century opera – it has an operatic convention-bound strategy of three staged acts, two intervals, an overture-prologue and an epilogue-coda – all in real time. We are 'going to the opera' in a big way. But I wonder if people picked up on these aspects, because they were so intimidated by the subject matter. The North American press complained vigorously about the multiple rape. They couldn't understand the seventeenth-century resonances of sacrifice and religiosity, and certainly could not make the twentieth-century connections. The film was made and shown at a time when officially sanctioned state policy in Bosnia legitimised the wholesale rape of Muslim women in a policy of deliberate humiliation.

A lot of the irony would seem to come from the film's theatrical structures, its Brechtian structures.
The stereotyped three estates of the audience, the aristocrats on stage 'fixing' the action, the deliberate depiction of the facts of religious trophy hunting, Prince Cosimo as a figure to unite the aims of Church and State – using a disingenuous simpleton idiot to achieve what is wanted. But I still don't think the film is ever going to get a decent showing. Like *The Belly of an Architect*, which had a very poor pattern of distribution in America, *The Baby of Mâcon* has now been sold to a powerless American operator, who has no resources or clout and is too eager to exploit its sensationalism.

That raises the whole question of the room for manoeuvre that you might have. You have lots of projects, but getting the funding and getting the films out, especially in a fairly tight, politically correct climate in a period of economic recession, must be difficult. What room for manoeuvre do you have?
I do feel that there are no censorship issues pushed in my direction by my producer, the most significant person in the equation. Provided I can come up with an idea which is conceived in full seriousness, and worked out with pragmatic thoroughness, he will try – and up till now he has succeeded – to find the money to support it; which, I believe, is a privileged relationship which very few directors can call upon. If you think about the collaborations since the Second World War between producers and directors, they've lasted for maybe four or five films but then, for all manner of reasons, they've changed, moved on, broken up. The relationship depends, of course, on certain strictures – we must make low-budget movies, otherwise we lose control. Most of these budgets are around the £2.5 million mark, which is mere pocket-money for the acting star in terms of commercial cinema – and inexpensive even for independent European or British cinema. The forms of censorship, if they exist, are of a different nature. Time is one. I would like to make movies that last longer than two hours. There's little space in 120 minutes to really develop an encyclopaedic idea. And many of the movies I would like to make are viewable as some form of encyclopaedia. For our next project, we hope to bite the bullet and make an eight-hour movie, with a version for the silver screen that will hopefully be seen in one session on some occasions. A television version is planned, possibly in sixteen parts – it is written in sixteen episodes – all of different lengths. We are keen, too, to make a double-volume CD-ROM, one to be ready on day one of the first cinema premiere and one to be ready as a post mortem, recapitulating and extending the fictions. We also hope to publish extensive relevant associated material on the Internet. Aesthetic and commercial suicide? We'll have to see.

In relation to the *Tulse Luper Suitcase*, which of the new technologies really excite you?
There is much of what we began to investigate on *The Pillow Book* that we wish to develop. Further afield, I would like to see if it might be possible to consider the idea of CD-ROM on OMNIMAX – screens so big they are frameless, beyond the periphery of vision. Scale seems to be a serious consideration in cinema. One of the great delights of a cinematic experience is that the images and the sound should be bigger and noisier than you are. But the technology for OMNIMAX CD-ROM doesn't exist yet and I don't think it will, because there's something contradictory about the idea, involving too great a financial stress between the single viewing characteristic of the CD-ROM and the multiple viewing characteristic of OMNIMAX. But I do believe that very soon cinema could suffer a massive split into private and public, because I'm not convinced that cinema is truly a social or sociable activity. It might be social when you go, it might be social when you come away, but for most people sitting there in the dark, it's an island experience, a one-to-

one private experience between you and the screen, and that is characteristic of all the new post-television technologies. Only one person at a time can use a CD-ROM. As a user, only one person at a time, sitting at the controls and the website monitor, can effectively use the Internet. So either cinema becomes a privately manipulated phenomenon, or it returns to its pre-history in the fairground and music hall, back to the notion of a viable social event with a lit auditorium, free and relaxed perambulation, and social interchange not made prohibitive by fixed seats and darkness – man is not a nocturnal animal, what's he doing sitting in the dark? So, real time, real 3D space communal activity, or the personalised screen, a wraparound affair courtesy of unreal reality operated at a one man/woman screen. I don't know how long this is going to take, but the cinema experience as we have known it – what I would call the *Casablanca* syndrome of the mid-twentieth century – will no longer satisfy our imagination. It's interesting that from the 1830s right up to the beginning of cinema, if you went to a theatrical, operatic or music-hall production, the lighting in the audience was almost as bright as the lighting on the stage. It's only subsequent to the invention of cinema that people have turned the lights down in the auditorium. We know from descriptions of nineteenth-century opera how it was as important to see your neighbours as it was the stage, so we can say quite genuinely that it was a social experience. Cinema buries the audience in darkness.

What about interactive media?

I confess that I'm not so sure anymore what this means. And in many conversations with the interactive media apologists I am not so sure that they know either. After all, reading literature is conceivably highly interactive and is no recent event. My intellectual interests would say, yes, choice and involvement are desirable and necessary with the maximum of interplay. I would also agree that our notion of the autocratic, Renaissance artist-figure as master-director should be eroded. We have a political system in the West which is broadly democratic and far from the oligarchies and monarchies of the Renaissance, so why haven't art and artists changed accordingly? But there are problems. I enjoy my subjectivity. And I enjoy experiencing other people's subjectivity. Is interactivity a threat to subjectivity? And can interactivity work en masse, in a crowd, catering to more than one imagination at once? And then, notions of interactivity which apparently give the audience control have all been predicated by the authors anyway. Eighty-four different endings to an interactive *War and Peace* will probably all have been invented by Tolstoy. What room is there really for free choice amounting to personal intervention? So, first of all, yes in principle; then a contradictory no, because I want to retain my subjectivity and enjoy the possibility of it and of the subjectivity of others without my, or other people's interference; and third, the practicalities of the idea – can we make it work? Even in a working democracy, in the long run I think the majority is probably often wrong, so there's a way in which the minorities could never be satisfied by a system that allows the majority to decide the outcome.

Do you go to the theatre?

Rarely. It embarrasses me. I have no ability to suspend my disbelief, or very little, in the theatre. Especially in purely illusionist theatre. And actors are always actors are always actors to me – even the best. I'm always surprised that theatre audiences are so uncritical.

Yet you use the theatre in your cinema. What is the attraction?

Control. I think it's the notion, first of all, of uses of artifice. My films are not particularly performance oriented, they do not permit the whole responsibility of the text and action to stay with the actor. They utilise *mise-en-scène* more thoroughly, are made deliberately more artificial by post-production, use actors as props, seek non-figuration and the abstract, or revel in artificial convention which in the end is anti-illusionist. I enjoy ceremony and ritual, inflexible traditions, etiquette, manners, hard won conventions, all of which do not essentially need 'performance' or narrative. I like the abstracted form of the catalogue and the list; organisation by preordained systems – number and alphabet, colour theory, equations – and from there myth and fable, reduced narratives and no narratives at all. Most of the movies I've made are catalogues of one sort or another. I enjoy variations on a theme, reprising, repeating, symmetry, coincidence – perhaps these are characteristics of musical structures. All of which is not the stuff of contemporary theatre and cinema. And theatre is traditionally text-driven, whereas my films try hard not to be and seek to be distant from the theatre-cinema of the English realist tradition – exemplified currently by Ken Loach and Mike Leigh but persistent generally in English cinema. I don't enjoy that English tradition which, I think, so easily becomes sheer actor self-regard. And there's a way in which I've always felt antagonistic and unhappy, even sometimes nauseous, about the notion of objective realism and so-called objective naturalism, which I think can be largely a political programme and not an aesthetic one. Besides, I don't really think it's possible in cinema. Employ a cameraman, employ an editor, and the subjectivities come rushing in and cannot and should not be denied. I do not subscribe at all to the idea that art should imitate life. The greatest plaudits for such an aesthetic revolve around praise for mimicry, the applause relying on how real, how observant it is – like marvelling at trompe l'oeil painting for its ability to make a likeness of life. In the end that seems to be mere cleverness, mere mimetic skill. And when the immediate praise for getting it right has passed, it suddenly looks tawdry, like the apparent impossibility now of mistaking a van Meegeren for a Vermeer. Have you seen *Bicycle Thieves* recently? Have you even seen *Saturday Night and Sunday Morning* recently? Supposedly, in their time, they were regarded as the height of realism but they already look curiously phoney now. So I have always presumed the Shakespearean way around this problem was the best: you go to the artificial end of things and you work backwards. My cinema is not a window on the world, it's not a door out onto the next-door neighbour's garden, it is a self-conscious and artificial construct. So let me try and tell you truths through artifice. As they say, you must first hold up a mirror to art before you can hold up a mirror to nature.

Is there any parallel to be drawn between your use of theatrical structures in the cinema and Brecht's use of cinema screens, projected text and so on in the theatre?

I'm sure there is. All the notions of alienation and self-conscious demonstration – presenting an artifice and relying on the perception of the audience to pick up the ideas through the artifice – I'm sure those are characteristics of my cinema. Like the theory of montage – demonstrate the idea of flying by showing an image of a bird and an image of a bird and an image of a man, instead of giving a man wings which we are never going to believe. There's a fashionable feeling, though, that mere mention of Brecht will bring on knowing groans of disapproval.

One thing that struck us in relation to *Prospero's Books*, but one could talk about it in relation to *The Pillow Book* as well, was the idea that here you are with a brand new medium, exploring a new technology, and the content you choose to foreground is an old technology, which is something right out of McLuhan. Is that an interesting paradox for you, the idea that in a sense the new technologies allow you to become more artisanal in cinema than you could have been previously?

Well, I would object very strongly to any modernist notion that there has to be a dramatic break with historical continuity. It's self-evident that we are nothing without memory, though I acknowledge that history is subjective. A general metaphor for the next film is that there is no such thing as history, there are only historians. I read a great deal of history and I enjoy sequence, chronology and continuity for their own sakes. I am dismayed that my own children will not be absolutely certain whether Henry VIII comes before Elizabeth or afterwards. People aren't even supposed to be interested in chronology anymore. It strikes me that if you don't have a chronology, how can you make use of all the other information? So the new technology should not be the broom that necessarily sweeps away the old – it can help one to understand the old better. A new language is used in *The Pillow Book* to discuss an old language – three thousand years of Oriental calligraphy seen through the vocabulary of what some have described as a television language. This can perhaps be exemplified as an anxiety. All the world's texts have been self-evidently made by the body, with the particular relationship of the head to the arm to the hand to the pen to the paper. With ubiquitous contemporary keyboards we have broken the body text link that started to decay with the printing press and accelerated with the typewriter. Is this just nostalgia? Is this just a reactionary notion? I don't think it is. One of the things I would forefront in all my films is that we must stay very aware of our own physicality. I started my life as a painter. You get a little dirty with the paint. Touch, texture, hand manipulation, smell. I spent years at art school when tachism, American Abstract Expressionism, the big physical painting gesture, a delight in mucky paint, was important. I was not interested in the romanticism of

some of that stuff – Yves Klein covering women in blue paint, taking things to exhibitionist lengths – but that notion of the physical world of creativity is very important. As a filmmaker I am removed from it. Everything is happening through a prism at a distance, projected at a distance, and now with television and all its techniques we are down to sound and sight. That's why we have to invent plastic substitute concepts of virtual reality. We've got so far away from the real reality, we experience an anxiety to get back to it again by mimicking it.

Perhaps it all started with the invention of the artificial frame passed on from painting to theatre to photograph to cinema to television – a frame that's getting tighter and tighter as it's passed on down the line of media. I'm sure it's a law of nature that eventually you tighten and concentrate to a point of exhaustion, so that there has to be a breaking, an explosion. We haven't maybe reached that yet, but there are warning signs everywhere. Even that amusing fact that computers cannot deal with the year 2000, with its row of three noughts, which could be a nice little fable about our failure to anticipate the consequences of our self-imposed text, then the best place for the text is back on the body. In the West we have painfully separated the notions of text and image, but Oriental ideograms still acknowledge the idea that the history of Japanese literature is also the history of Japanese painting. They are bound together but we in the West have somehow made this decision to separate them, especially in England. If you are a painter you are not supposed to be a writer. If you are a writer you are not supposed to be a painter. You'd imagine cinema to be the ideal place to marry these two things together, yet it hasn't done so. In cinema, images are enslaved to the text. So the notion of picking up the ideogram, the hieroglyph, the Oriental character as a possible template for cinema could be a very interesting idea.

What about the question of the local? Are you optimistic about the kinds of globalism we're seeing now? Your own practice is becoming much more global in the sense that *The Pillow Book*, for example, has very different subjects and concerns from those of, say, *The Draughtsman's Contract*. Which is partly about a successful practice that takes you to all these places and offers you new technologies that are not available to those people who are stuck at the local. In that sense you are privileged. But under the veneer of the universalism of the global village, are we actually losing the idea of the local?

Maybe we are. I'm not sure whether this is good or bad. English filmic traditions seem to me to be tedious in their localness. But seeking the global can lead to blandness and banality because of little and insufficient knowledge of the particular. To the irritation of many distributors, a lot of the Japanese and Oriental languages in *The Pillow Book* are not translated. This might be cavalier but I'm quite sure that in three decades time, kids in Toronto and Chicago will never hear a foreign language, which is obviously disastrous to their placement in the world and leads to the demise of cultural ideas. Like depleting the South American rainforests of species by monoculture, it might even lead to a total breakdown of the whole cultural system. With *The Pillow Book* I wanted audiences just to listen – there wasn't much chance of their understanding all the meanings – because people don't seem to want to listen anymore to the sheer cadences and rhythms of these strange-sounding, foreign languages which are so beautiful and so fascinating. Global and local, home and abroad, I don't know how to answer this question with any absolute conviction, but I don't want to be particularly associated with English filmmaking that seems now to be investigating the minutiae of working class opinion, attitudes, habits, prejudices, in the way the middle classes were scrutinised earlier in the century. Seeking other areas, what do I give up? Do I give up my Englishness? My movies are very French. My design team used to be Dutch. We do really feel as though we are good Europeans on an European enterprise. I'm Welsh by origin and the Welsh, with their minority language, are better Europeans than the English anyway. But this is a problem, remembering the David Puttnam movie credo, where we were supposed to be Anglo-American, producing films for the most part that were banal, never as good as what the Americans could do, and somehow bowdlerising or pastiching English culture for tourist appeal. So I don't really have an answer to your question. I will continue to push where I want to push and I will just have to suffer the consequences. Our next movie starts in the Utah desert looking for lost Mormon townships and ends up looking for Coleridge's Kubla Khan in Manchuria. Is that local?

We've talked about *The Tulse Luper Suitcase* in terms of the media it uses, but what is the film about?

You may know the story of Raoul Wallenberg who performed a sort of Schindler's List in Budapest for the Hungarian Jews against the Fascists. What interested me was that this apparent Christ-like figure on the last day of the war disappears into Russia. Nobody sees him go. Occasionally there is an exchange of prisoners across Checkpoint Charlie and somebody comes out and says, 'I saw this man who spoke with a Swedish accent polishing his shoes in a Siberian gulag'. Six months later, another sighting, another story. The saint becomes deified as the missing martyred political prisoner. My protagonist, Tulse Luper, is no real Wallenberg, but he goes through a series of prisons which are analogous to Wallenberg's ever-disappearing Russian act – though not in Russia. He starts his prison career in 1936 in America. We travel to Europe in 1938-39, and the causes of imprisonment are certainly to do with the con-

veniences and hazards of war but also with private loves and enmities. He is jailed for ostensibly different reasons and makes a picaresque journey that ends up in the East. We finish towards the end of the Cultural Revolution in China in 1969. Prisons don't always have walls and bars. They can be prisons of obsession, fascination, interest and ambition.

The hero is a writer; he writes on his prison walls. The film, even in eight hours, will not be able to tell you all that he writes, but the CD-ROM may very well do. There are ninety-two suitcases that have to be packed and unpacked. Ninety-two is the atomic number of uranium in this Cold War movie. Not surprisingly, the hero doesn't want to be found in the end. He's perfectly happy. He doesn't want the walls to come down. We become intensely interested in our own obsessions, fascinations and neuroses. And to throw people off the scent, to mystify and misdirect his lovers of whom he has a great many, both masculine and feminine, he packs suitcases. And other people pack suitcases on his behalf. Some of them are deliberately phoney. People find them all over the world and these will be described in detail on the Internet. So even before the film is made we itemise, listing enthusiastically, all the objects. There's a suitcase of Vatican pornography, a suitcase of dead dogs, bloodied Romanian sewing needles, cork frogs, alphabetically arranged alcohol, fake poems, guns and roses, apples and pears, spent fireworks, dungarees, lost Julio Romano drawings . . . and some of them are just toiletries and clean shirts and toothpaste. Ultimately, everyone realises there is one final suitcase to be reckoned with – the final Tulse Luper Suitcase.

So the film runs on two levels. There's the history of the ever-disappearing Tulse Luper, who becomes more wraithlike as he disappears further and further into more and more obscure prisons, and there's the history, transport, identification – that is getting stronger and stronger – of the suitcases. Ultimately we find the last suitcase, and all is revealed. By now it's become almost like an iconic art object and, with much solemnity amongst selected curators and lecturers and experts who have been commenting about this history of Luper all the way through the film, there's a grand opening of the suitcase, rather like the way they open mummies before the television cameras. Everybody waits to see what's in the final suitcase . . . and I'm not going to tell you.

FILMOGRAPHY

1966   Train, *5 mins*
       Tree, *16 mins*

1967   Revolution, *8 mins*
       5 Postcards from Capital Cities, *35 mins*

1969   Intervals, *7 mins*

1971   Erosion, *27 mins*

1973   H is for House, *10 mins (re-edited in 1978)*

1975   Windows, *4 mins*
       Water, *5 mins*
       Water Wrackets, *12 mins*

1976   Goole by Numbers, *40 mins*

1977   Dear Phone, *17 mins*

1978   1-100, *4 mins*
       A Walk Through H, *41 mins, BFI*
       Vertical Features Remake, *45 mins, Arts Council of Great Britain*

1979   Zandra Rhodes, *15 mins, Central Office of Information*

1980   The Falls, *185 mins, BFI*

1981   Act of God, *25 mins, Thames TV*

1982   The Draughtsman's Contract, *108 mins, BFI and Channel Four Television*

1983   Four American Composers *(Robert Ashley, John Cage, Philip Glass, Meredith Monk), 55 mins, Channel Four Television*

1984   Making a Splash, *25 mins Channel Four and Media Software*

1985   Inside Rooms – 26 Bathrooms, *25 mins, Channel Four (video)*
       A TV Dante Canto 5, *10 mins (pilot)*

1986   A Zed & Two Noughts, *112 mins, BFI, Film Four International, Allarts Enterprises and Artificial Eye*

1987   The Belly of an Architect, *105 mins, Callender Company, Film Four International, British Screen, Sacis, Hemdale*

1988   Drowning by Numbers, *108 mins, Allarts Enterprises, Film Four International, Elsevier Vendex Film*
       Fear of Drowning, *26 mins, Channel Four Television*
       Death in the Seine, *44 mins, Erato Films, Mikros Image, La Sept, Allarts TV Productions*

1989   A TV Dante Cantos 1-8, *10 mins x 8, VPRO, Elsevier Vendex Film, Channel Four Television*
       Hubert Bals Handshake, *5 mins, Allarts Enterprises*
       The Cook, the Thief, His Wife and Her Lover, *120 mins, Allarts Cook, Erato Films*

1991   Prospero's Books, *123 mins, Allarts, Cinea, Camera One, Penta Film, Elsevier Vendex Film, Film Four International, VPRO, Canal+, NHK*
       M is for Man, Music, Mozart, *30 mins, BBC, AVRO, Artifax*

1992   Rosa, *15 mins, La Monnaie de Munt, Rosas*
       Darwin, *52 mins, Telemax Les Éditions Audiovisuelles, Allarts, Antenne 2, Channel Four, RAI 2, Telepool, Time Warner*

1993   The Baby of Mâcon, *118 mins, Allarts Enterprises, UGC-La Sept, Cine Electra II, Channel Four Television, Filmstiftung Nordrhein Westfalen, Canal+*

1994   The Stairs, Geneva, *100 mins, Apsara*

1996   The Pillow Book, *123 mins, Kasander & Wigman, Woodline Films, Alpha Films, Channel Four Films, Studio Canal+, Delux Productions*

OPERA

1994   Rosa, A Horse Drama, *Opera in 12 scenes, 80 mins, music by Louis Andriessen, Musiektheater, Amsterdam, 10 performances*

Day 2
22 February 1996
Country Kitchen

EXHIBITIONS

Curatorial

1991 The Physical Self
Boymans-van Beuningen Museum, Rotterdam, Netherlands

1992 Hundert Objekte zeigen die Welt – 100 Objects to Represent the World
Akademie der Bildenden Künste, Vienna, Austria
Le Bruit des Nuages – Flying Out of This World
The Louvre, Paris, France

1993 Watching Water
Palazzo Fortuny, Venice Biennale, Italy
Some Organising Principles
Glynn Vivian Art Gallery, Swansea, UK
The Audience of Mâcon
Ffoto Gallery, Cardiff, UK

1994 The Stairs/Geneva: The Location
Geneva, Switzerland

1995 The Stairs/Munich: Projection
Munich, Germany

1996 In the Dark *(Part of* Spellbound: Art and Film*)*
Hayward Gallery, London, UK
Cosmology at the Piazza del Popolo, a history of the Piazza from Nero to Fellini using light and sound
Rome, Italy

Solo Shows

1988 *Broad Street Gallery, Canterbury, England*

1989 *Arcade, Carcassonne, France*
Palais de Tokyo, Paris, France

1990 *Nicole Klagsbrun Gallery, New York, USA*
Australia Centre of Contemporary Art, Melbourne, Australia
Ivan Dougherty Gallery, College of Fine Arts, Australia
The University of New South Wales, Paddington, Australia
Cirque Divers, Liège, Belgium
Shingawa Space T33, Tokyo, Japan
Altium, Fukoa, Japan
Dany Keller Galerie, Munich, Germany
Video Galleriet, Copenhagen, Denmark
Kunsthallen Brandts Klædefabrik, Odense, Denmark
Galerie Xavier Hufkens, Brussels, Belgium

1991 *Watermans Gallery, Brentford, England*
City Art Centre, Dublin, Ireland

1992 *Gesellschaft für Aktuelle Kunst, Bremen, Germany*
Nicole Klagsbrun Gallery, New York, USA

1994 *Arizona State University Art Museum, Tempe, Arizona, USA*
Gesellschaft für Max Reinhardt Forschung, Salzburg, Austria

1995 *Centre PasquART, Biel-Bienne, Switzerland*
Nicole Klagsbrun Gallery, New York, USA
Dany Keller Galerie, Munich, Germany

1996 *Le Case d'Arte, Milan, Italy*
Galerie Fortlaan 17, Ghent, Belgium

OPPOSITE
'In the Dark', Spellbound, Hayward Gallery, London, 1996

BIBLIOGRAPHY

1984 Greenaway, Peter, Meurtre dans un jardin anglais/The Draughtsman's Contract, L'Avant-Scène Cinéma 333, Octobre, 47-117 [English/French]

1986 Greenaway, Peter, A Zed & Two Noughts, Faber and Faber, London

1987 Caux, Daniel, Michel Field, Florence de Meredieu, Philippe Pilard, Michael Nyman, Peter Greenaway, Dis Voir, Paris [French]

1988 Greenaway, Peter, The Belly of an Architect, Faber and Faber, London

Greenaway, Peter, Drowning by Numbers, Faber and Faber, London

Greenaway, Peter, Fear of Drowning by Numbers: Règles du jeu, (trans) Barbara Dent, Danièle Rivière, Bruno Alcala, Dis Voir, Paris [English/French]

1989 Greenaway, Peter, The Cook, the Thief, His Wife and Her Lover, Dis Voir, Paris

1990 Greenaway, Peter, Papers/Papiers, (French trans) Guillemette Belleteste, Dis Voir, Paris [English/French]

1991 Greenaway, Peter, Prospero's Books, Chatto & Windus, London

1992 Greenaway, Peter, Le Bruit des nuages/Flying Out of This World, Éditions de la Réunion des musées nationaux, Paris [English/French]

Greenaway, Peter, Hundert Objekte zeigen die Welt/ Hundred Objects to Represent the World, Verlag Gerd Hatje, Stuttgart [English/German]

Greenaway, Peter, The Physical Self, Museum Boymans-van Beuningen, Rotterdam [English/Dutch]

Greenaway, Peter, Prospero's Subjects, Kamakura, Yobisha, Japan [no text]

Berthin-Scaillet, Agnès (ed), Peter Greenaway: Fête et défaite du corps. L'Avant-Scène Cinéma 417/418, December 1992-January 1993 [French]

1993 Barchfeld, Christiane, Filming by Numbers: Peter Greenaway. Ein Regisseur zwischen Experimentalkino und Erzählkino,

Gunter Narr Verlag, Tübingen [German]

Denham, Laura, The Films of Peter Greenaway, Minerva Press, London

Greenaway, Peter, The Audience of Mâcon, Wales Film Council; Ffotogallery, Cardiff [English/Welsh]

Greenaway, Peter, The Falls, Dis Voir, Paris

Greenaway, Peter, Rosa, Dis Voir, Paris

Greenaway, Peter, Some Organising Principles, Glynn Vivian Art Gallery, Swansea [English/Welsh]

Greenaway, Peter, Watching Water, Electa, Milan

Prof Luca Massimo Barbero, Peter Greenaway: Watching Water, (trans) David Stanton, Electa, Milan [English/Italian]

1994 Greenaway, Peter, The Baby of Mâcon, (French trans) Christophe Marchand-Kiss, Dis Voir, Paris [French]

Greenaway, Peter, The Stairs/Geneva: The Location, Merrell Holberton, London [English/French]

1995 Greenaway, Peter, The Stairs/Munich: Projection, Merrell Holberton, London [English/German]

De Gaetano, Domenico, Il Cinema di Peter Greenaway, Lindau, Turin [Italian]

Gorostiza, Jorge, Peter Greenaway, Ediciones Cátedra, Madrid [Spanish]

Kramer, Detlef, Peter Greenaways Filme, Verlag JB Metzler [German]

Lüdeke, Jean, Die Schönheit des Schrecklichen: Peter Greenaway und seine Filme, Bergisch Gladbach: Gustav Lübbe Verlag [German]

Steinmetz, Leon, and Peter Greenaway, The World of Peter Greenaway, Journey Editions, Boston

Thau, Carsten, and Anders Troelsen, Filmen som verdensteater – omkring Peter Greenaway, KLIM.NSU, Arhus [Danish]

1996 Bencivenni, Alessandro, and Anna Samueli, Peter Greenaway, il cinema delle idee. Recco, Le Mani, Genova [Italian]

Woods, Alan, Being Naked – Playing Dead: The Art of Peter Greenaway, Manchester University Press, Manchester